Dedicated to

Brigid Sturgess 1964-2015

My first cousin & friend

ACKNOWLEDGEMENTS

Thanks to Steven & Niamh of Original Writing for helping put this project together. To my sister-in-law, Gene Browner, and Auntie Maura, for having a look at the manuscript; my brother Gerry for all the photocopying. To Christine Moynihan for her painting – Fort Pond (front cover). The back cover is a wall tile that I purchased on the Greek island of Ios in the early eighties and has moved from place to place with me since.

I am forever grateful to former teachers and mentors – Colm Keegan; Eileen Casey; Mia Gallagher; members of the Eblana Writers' Group on Fitzwilliam Square and the Café Writers who meet in the Bridge Café, Bray, County Wicklow, every Tuesday. My students in the 'Over 50's Activities Group'; Kill o' the Grange Oral History class and Loughlinstown Creative Writers, who are the best teachers.

To my family and friends who have always supported my writing, especially – Maura & Tom Cross; Alice Larkin; Brid Claffey; Una Halligan, Marie Scully for her great ideas and JJ Bunyan who gave me one great big idea. And to Regina Browner who told me about the Winter Warmer Competition in which my story, *Me & Suzy*, received third prize and led to the idea for this collection.

A big thank you to my cousin, Brendan Browner, whose December newsletter contained a lot of the images in the poem, *Something Wrong with this Picture* and to Mary McCormack for allowing me present HerStory to her transition students in St. Aloysius College, Carrigtwohill.

YOU COULD'VE BEEN SOMEONE

Stories Memories & Poems

Frances Browner

ORIGINAL WRITING

ISBNS
PARENT : 978-1-78237-886-0
EPUB: 978-1-78237-887-7
MOBI: 978-1-78237-888-4
PDF: 978-1-78237-889-1

A CIP catalogue for this book is available from the National Library.

Published by ORIGINAL WRITING LTD., Dublin, 2015.
Printed by CLONDALKIN GROUP, Glasnevin, Dublin 11

In anticipation, thank you Sally Ann and Naomi for your help at the launch.

Last, but not least, thank you to Sean Nolan and Phil Murphy of *Ireland's Own* for publishing my work and to Cliodhna Ni Anluain and Aoife Nic Cormaic of RTE for broadcasting it on radio.

And to all of you who have read these pieces in the past and told me that you liked them.

I am just going to write because I cannot help it

– *Charlotte Bronte*

Contents

Short Stories

Just Memories

Poems

SHORT STORIES

ME & SUZY

The black patent cover had started to crack, the tarnished gold clasp wobbling. I pried the first few pages apart, could barely make out the faded words *to Clare from Agnes* on the inside front cover. Underneath was my list of *'things to do before I'm 21'*. Number 7 was *get engaged*; and 8 – *marry*. Agnes had never longed for anything at all that I knew of.

We'd been friends since our first day in the Dominican. Had bonded over babies - our mother's, not our own.

Mam had announced in August that there was another on the way, her eighth. I'd spent the summer reading the Glaxo Mother & Baby book and knew what awful things women had men do to them to beget babies. I was starting Secondary School in September and wondered how I would tell my new friends.

"Me Ma's having a baby." Agnes ran into the classroom, bursting with the news and I was delighted when the stick-like little thing with the stringy blond hair took the seat beside mine in the front desk.

"Where do they do it?" I mustered up the courage to ask her one day, while Miss St. Ledger droned on about the square on the hypotenuse.

"Do what?"

"You know . . ." I shrugged. "It?"

"Oh," Agnes said, her bony chest swelling with importance. "In bed."

Bed?

I was as bewildered by the location as I had been by the act. Meanwhile, I was holding out for my mother to produce a girl to level out the sides in my family's battle of the sexes. Agnes wanted a brother for her and her six sisters.

Two Little Boys we sang along with Rolf Harris that summer, rolling the prams over the pebbles on Killiney beach, Agnes searching for flat ones to skim along the teal grey water.

"I want to be called Suzy from now on," she announced in Second Year.

We were on a Retreat with the school, in a convent in County Wicklow, our bags bulging with sweets for the midnight feasts, obsessing about honeymoons and wedding nights and the strange things couples got up to in bed. Me and Suzy were still in hairbands and ankle socks while some of our classmates already had pimples and handbags. They spent ages in the Confession Box and reappeared gushing with the Priest's questions. Had they ever felt a tingling in their breasts when passing a group of boys was the one that me and Suzy had mulled over the most.

After our Inter Cert results, we went to Sandycove for a swim and met up with lads, the first we'd ever chatted. The one I clapped eyes on was already taken, whereas a quiet blond boy took a shine to Suzy. "It's a lovely name," he said shyly, the blood rushing to his face. She shot me a look and said, "Thanks."

He'd meet her at the gate after school and I'd watch them from the bus window, holding hands all the way up the Glasthule Road. They spent Saturdays in Dun Laoghaire eating chips in the Wimpy Bar, Sundays on the strand at Killiney, kissing. Her lips were sore from the kissing, she said. And at the Fifth Year retreat it was Suzy who spent forever inside the Confessional and not a word about it after.

She disappeared for most of Sixth Year and never sat her Leaving Cert. There was an empty space in the desk beside me and ours was no longer the Suzy & Clare class. We heard she'd been sent off to boarding school, to her Granny down the country, to an aunt in England.

"I had a baby," she told me one day in August when I found her standing on the doorstep. "And then I gave it up," she said.

I ushered her into the sitting-room where the pile of books I'd been reading all summer had been scattered across the floor by younger siblings.

"Never saw me fella since," said Suzy.

I could hear the cry of gulls, the flip flap of the waves, the plop, plop, plop of my stones dropping to the bottom of the sea, the swish shoo of Suzy's skimming along the top of the water.

"Took all me tablets in one go," she was saying. "Had to have me stomach pumped. They kept me in for a few months." She took a deep breath. "For therapy."

"I like your eye shadow," was all I could think of to say. But, Suzy wasn't listening. "They made me write in a diary every day," she said. "Pure torture it was, jotting down all me thoughts and feelings."

That first Christmas, her eyes were dancing and her hands shaking, as she handed me the crumpled paper bag and said, "I bought you a present." The first one I ever got from my first ever best friend. I pulled out a five-year diary, with a black patent cover and a shiny gold clasp.

"Bye Suzy," I said, as she walked away that day.

"You can call me Agnes now." She clicked the gate closed.

I stood at the door until she disappeared around the end of our Avenue, the whole time hoping she'd turn around and find me there, waving.

I skimmed through the diary later . . . *Me and Suzy mitched from school . . . Me and Suzy went to Prudence & the Pill . . . Me and Suzy picked for throw 'n duck team . . . Me and Suzy reading The Kiss of Paris . . . Me and Suzy bought our first pair of tights in Dunnes* . . . All of the events of our lives were recorded there; not a word about what we thought, or felt.

I ended up in a Solicitor's office after, while Agnes settled into a job in the Slipper Factory. We met men eventually and married them. For me, it was late-in-life, people said, too late for children anyhow and Agnes didn't have any more that I heard of. We pass each other by on a Dun Laoghaire street sometimes and I brace myself for what I will call her if she stops to speak. But, she potters along, shoulders stooped, face fixed on the floor and my heart sinks every time, like a stone.

3rd place Winter Warmer competition 2014

THREE-LEGGED DOG

It was the summer of seventy-six, a song would say, the year Phil and I sat for our Leaving Certificate. After which we cycled down to County Wexford on a June afternoon. Now, they're shaggin' off to Shagaluf to celebrate the end of exams, but for us it was to be an equally great adventure, we hoped. On the seventy-mile excursion from Dun Laoghaire, the N11 not yet completed, we took the old roads, as well as the odd stretch of dual carriageway. The outgoing journey shorter than the one coming back.

"When you see The Goal Post, you'll know you're there," Dad had said. And there it was, a ramshackle shop cum public house, with a three-legged dog snarling at the door. While Phil kept him at bay with his foot, I tackled the messages. We had a frying pan so sausages it was for the tea and a great big doorstep of a loaf, spongy to touch, topped with a thick black crust. As we freewheeled down the rickety road to the campsite, the dog pursued us, snapping at my ankles, causing me to jam on the brakes, somersault over the handlebars and land on my bottom in a bed of nettles.

"Eejit," said Phil, shaking his head from side to side, while I eased myself upright and the dog scarpered back up the hill.

We pitched the tent in minutes and when it looked reasonably secure, we raced towards the beach and stripped off our outer clothes, the trunks underneath not the best protection against a saddle, or nettle sting. The salt water would soon see to both.

Dad had taught me to swim when I was seven, taking me out on his back in Seapoint, dropping me in the water and shouting me back to shore. He had completed the Shannon Swim as a young lad in Limerick, but none of his children excelled at the sport. If you'd call it sport.

We were having great sport that afternoon, Phil and I, the place packed with possibility. The water was calm, the weather balmy, as it is when you look back, and we hadn't a care, our futures stretching out beyond the horizon. University, jobs, marriage, kids, sitting around the table of a Good Friday night drinking wine with our spouses and wondering if we'd done the right thing?

"We have company." Phil popped up out of the water, tilting his head towards the strand.

And there, sure enough, were three girls, slightly older than us, discarding their clothes. Phil sucked in his breath and slowly exhaled. The girls were giggling, slapping themselves with towels, chasing one another across the fine sugary sand, as girls do. We continued swimming, our heads cocked to the side, ignoring them, as boys do.

They ran into the water screeching, dove under its glassy surface and disappeared. I held my breath, until they reappeared seconds later, looking like seal pups, their hair sleek, heads smooth and round. And then they swam past us, treading the water gracefully with their long limbs, not even glancing in our direction.

"Can't understand why people do that," Phil said.

"What?" I asked, between gasps for breath.

"Swim so far out to sea like that, instead of parallel to the shore."

"What's the difference?" I struggled to find the sandy floor with my feet.

"It's safer," he said.

I started to plough back through the wet sand, gathering tiny stones between my toes, reaching the water's edge with relief. I'd had enough, of the conversation and the swim.

"I mean . . ." Phil followed me. He wouldn't let up. He was like that when he had a point he thought worth making. "I bet you can swim around the whole circumference of Ireland, all the time only ten yards from the coast line."

"I bet you're right," I said, looking back at the girls, who were quite a distance away, still shrieking, their shiny heads bobbing up and down, their hands now waving at me.

We returned to the campsite, famished, only to discover that I had lost the sausages. They were either still on the shop counter or had fallen out of the rucksack during my cartwheel over the bushes. Probably devoured by the three-legged dog by now, and as our budget didn't stretch to another pound, we dined on fresh bread and cider.

We talked about the summer, how many honours we were expecting in the Leaving Cert, University in the autumn and what we'd do after that. Travel the world maybe? Or even *Eurorail*? We wandered around the village later, scratching our backsides, aimlessly looking for girls, drinking copious amounts of cider, arriving back at the tent in time to pass out, drunk.

"Hello, hello." I woke with a start and saw a light flashing in my face, a bulky beast of a man filling the entrance to the tent. "Have you seen any girls?" he said.

"No," I said, blinking. "We've been looking for some ourselves."

"Pathetic," said Phil, from the sleeping-bag.

"Smart Alec," said the beast, flashing the light around the tent. "There's girls missing. Have you seen them?"

Phil sat up, rubbing his eyes with his fist. "Well, actually," he said to the flashlight. "We did see three girls swimming earlier."

"What do you mean by earlier? And whereabouts?" The man hunkered down so that his face was directly in front of ours. It was then I noticed the hat. A Guard's hat he had and a badge on his chest glistening in the dark.

There was another voice behind him, "Tell 'em come out ou' a that tent so's we can talk to 'em properly." With a swish of the flashlight, we were ushered outside. "Bring us to where you last saw 'em," we were told.

We pulled on our jeans and runners, zipped up our anoraks and stumbled through the field as far as the wooden walkway, now covered in sand. A cold breeze was blowing; the air filled with seaweed, salt, a distant sewer. The two Guards stomping behind us, the old crescent moon a bright yellow banana in the black sky. We lumbered along the strand until we came to the spot, but I had seen it long before that. The three bundles of clothes, a red jumper sticking out, a blue blouse with a print of pink flowers, brown leather sandals thrown nonchalantly in a heap, the three striped towels lying like flags on the white sand. I could feel them flap against their lithe bodies, hear their giggles, see their heads like seals poking out of the water.

"That's it, Sir," said Phil to the Guards. "That's their clothes and last time we saw them, they were out there . . ." he pointed to an obscure location at the end of his finger. "Swimming . . . out there, in the sea, the three of them."

"And have you seen 'em since?"

"No, Sir."

"Did they look like they were in difficulty?"

"No, Sir."

"Don't you have a tongue?" One of them pucked me in the rear end with the flashlight.

"No," I said, still scratching.

"No, what?"

"No, they looked fine," I said. "Not in any difficulty at all."

"We didn't see a thing after that," said Phil.

"Christ," said one of the Guards. "We'll have to call in the Coast Guards.

They escorted us back to the tent, where we sat, shivering. "Jesus," was all Phil could say. An hour or so later, when the sun was streaking the sky a garish pink, we saw an army of Guards, Coast Guards and Life Guards, marching towards the beach.

By midday, the whole town was involved in the search. The girls were twentyish, we overheard. Down from Dublin for the day, they said, pronouncing the word Dublin with venom. Their car was found abandoned in a field with a Scotch terrier yapping in the front seat, the animal now gnawing at their clothes, running around in circles, creating a commotion with the sand.

The girls' families arrived and their cries had a plaintive ring to them, primeval, as raw as the wind in our faces, the sound of the seagulls. The search intensified. Boats trawled the water, divers dunk in and out of the waves, which were rougher than the day before, as if on purpose. Searchers hacked the bulrushes, the marram grass and the large expanse of wasteland skirting the cove.

Phil and I weren't sure what we were looking for exactly, but we loped along after them trying to be of some use.

Every now and then, we stopped for a break at The Goal Post. Mugs of hot tea and plates of Marietta biscuits were passed around. Most people too stunned to eat, except us. A little butter would have been nice, to sandwich the biscuits together, so as we could lick the creamy yellow bits oozing out through their pinprick holes.

That night, because of torrential rain, the owner insisted that we sleep on the shop floor. We spread our sleeping bags out on the brown puckered lino and eyed the glass case of chocolate bars that would be at our disposal.

"Make up for the sausages," Phil whispered.

Two shop assistant cum lounge girls eyed us from behind the counter, tittering. The shopkeeper locked the main door, the sweets cabinet and the safe, keys jangling from his side pocket, a machine gun of farts ricocheting against his trousers, leaving a stench like boiled cabbage water in his wake. The girls fell into convulsions and fled. Phil and I stuffed our anorak sleeves into our mouths. In the pub, the terrier was still yapping; the three-legged mongrel stuck with us, whining.

The next day, the bodies were found. Three mounds were placed on the strand covered with white sheets. Our tent had collapsed overnight. Sodden rucksacks floated in a foot of water along with the frying pan, empty cider bottles and crusts of bread. We packed quickly and I rang Dad from the local telephone kiosk.

"Don't worry," he said. "It's forecast sunshine for the afternoon." And sure enough, as we pushed our bicycles up the hill and out of town, the sun crept from behind the clouds. We passed The Goal Post and saw the three-legged mutt humping the fluffy white terrier at the side of the shop. We held up our fists and shouted 'hurray.'

"Glad someone got their sweets," said Phil.

The sun was beating down on us, as we cycled through Enniscorthy and Gorey, on past the purple hills, the yellow gorse, the fields of lavender, along the dual carriageway at

Kilmacanogue, in the back road by Shankhill, up the hill at Killiney, down through Dalkey and on to Dun Laoghaire and the rest of our lives.

"It doesn't matter," I insist at the annual Good Friday night gathering, when Phil and the women contemplate whether it would have been better to live life first and then settle down to marriage and kids, or the way we did it, the other way around. "Things would have worked out the same in the end."

Sometimes in the summer though, I could be driving home along the seafront, or sitting out the back of an evening, or lying in bed after sunrise waiting for the alarm to go off, and a picture will flash before my eyes.

I'll see a wide expanse of water, clear as glass, three seals' heads bouncing up and down against the horizon and three pairs of arms waving frantically at me.

Or sometimes, I'll just see a three-legged dog.

March 2013

BACK TO BOOTAGH

The train pulls into Derry on a warm June afternoon. Passengers disembark and are on their way. Nobody notices the small sixtyish woman struggling with a suitcase. She crosses Foyle Street, passes the Guildhall and heads for the bus depot, depending on memory to get there. The city is noisy, the people pale and darkly dressed, everyone looking the same, all knowing d'other. She secures a ticket for the Swilly bus. Lizzie Doherty is on her way back to Bootagh for the first time in forty years.

"Don't forget to write," Dada had said the day she left, "and say the Rosary." And every week without fail, she had despatched a flimsy airmail letter until there was no one at the other end to receive it. His purple beads had slipped between her fingers most nights, while she pictured him kneeling on the flag floor at home, head bent, cap in hand, muttering the same prayer she did. She felt for them in her pocket now, as the lilac hills rose up around her. In New York it was the towering buildings that hid the sun but, you always knew it was there.

She had liked it well enough at the start. Any amount of fresh faces, honey brown, yellowish, boot polish black; then there was the loud laughter out of them, the melodious voices. She had a job with her Lady, girls to pal with, a social life even and a boy, once. It was in latter years that the days stretched, with memories reeling like a slideshow in her head, the news trickling from home and then stopping altogether. She couldn't read the letters anyhow, had to pay a man to do it, and had to pay him again to write back.

"You can be anyone you like." Her Lady would look at her in the mirror, as Lizzie brushed her long copper hair, the crystal perfume bottles glistening in her green eyes when she asked, "Do you know that?"

"I do," Lizzie would say, even though she didn't. The only thing she'd learnt on the small Donegal farm was that work was the way; that prayer and humility would guarantee her salvation.

"The meek shall inherit the earth," her mother would remark, her hands buried in flour or sudsy water, her skin crinkled like crepe. Yet, she must have been a young woman when Lizzie left, only in her forties by Lizzie's reckoning now.

But, it's the bullies that get what they want, Lizzie learnt. Stepping forward and stomping on you, trampling your toes at a dance to take your man. She'd asked Peggy to mind Mikey when she stayed home to care for her Lady. When the green was fading from her eyes like the leaves on Fifth Avenue come fall, the metallic shine from her hair.

"No good turn goes unpunished," Peggy said, her round body rattling with laughter when Mikey held out his hand to her in the Roseland Ballroom, ignoring Lizzie like she wasn't there, her heart falling to the floor. Nevertheless, she remained rigid at the wall, forcing a smile, her head high, as Mama had taught her. Never let anyone know you're hurtin' she'd say and Lizzie never did after that.

She heard it wasn't a good match. She remembered his hands, callous from hard work, but tender too around her thin waist and thought of what they'd done to Peggy. It didn't bring her any ease. "What goes around comes around," Mama would say, kneading the dough into a cake, scrubbing the spuds, sprinkling meal at the hens. But, by the time things come around, they don't matter anymore.

The bus stops at the top of the lane. The road is matted with grass and weeds, the bushes overgrown. There's not the roar of a cow, the cluck of a hen, not the cry of the corncrake, no human voice. Not even a bee buzzing.

She shuffles along, pulling the bag behind her, all she has to show for forty years. There was no use collecting things. She'd never lived in anything bigger than a box and sometimes had to share that. And they'd needed the money at home.

Dada had walked her up this *boreen* the day she left, Honora and Kate skipping behind them, Dada humming to himself and Lizzie daydreaming about Ned from the night before. Maire the Glen had organized her Bottling, one in a string of emigrant wakes that time. "I'll not be long after ya," her friend had promised. They'd danced to Mad Andy's melodeon and Fitzer's French fiddle and at one stage she and Maire's brother, Ned, were whirling around the kitchen at such a speed, they nearly fell into the fire. Oh, there was such banter after that, with Ned flapping the smoke from her peuce taffeta skirt.

"Maybe it's that you want to keep her here," Mad Andy said, manoeuvring the melodeon back and forth across his knee. Lizzie's face burnt from the idea of it, and from the way Ned held her in the swing like he'd never let her go. She'd no notion of him before that.

By the time they reached the end of the lane the next day, the air full of turf smoke and wet straw, the blackberries purple on her lips, Dada now singing *Red Sails in the Sunset* in full voice, Honora and Kate squabbling over who would see the bus first, she'd got to thinking, what if I stayed? What if I turned around this minute and went back? Thoughts that haunted her the next forty years. That and wishing she'd given Ned a look or a smile, some sort of sign that her mind could be changed.

"Wishing is easy after the fact," her Lady said. "I'm going to send you to school. Get you an education, a proper job, which will lead to a good marriage, a home of your own."

"But, I have a job," Lizzie said. "And a home here."

"You'll be wanting one of your own someday," her Lady said. "And, even after you marry, you should always retain some independence." She touched the side of her mouth where it quivered.

Lizzie often wondered about the swollen lips, the bruised patches around her eyes. Men's cruelty knew no boundaries, crossed all classes.

"Your life is on another course now," her Lady had said when Lizzie first told her about Mikey. She was lying in bed, her hair in strings on the pillow. "Grasp it with both hands."

She never got a chance to tell her about Peggy grasping him instead, never got to ask her what she should do next. Her Gentleman closed up the house and gave Lizzie notice. Dada said she'd be as welcome home as the flowers in May, but she'd wait another while. She couldn't go back the way she came, one arm longer than d'other. In another two years, she'd have enough stored to set herself up in Donegal town; she could have a high-school diploma, be able to get an office job in Derry. Marry Ned, maybe.

He'd never bothered with anyone, Mama had said in one of her letters, preferred to remain a bachelor boy and stop with his mother. "He often asks about you," Mama had Honora or Kate write down the words.

Lizzie moved into a railroad apartment. A chain of rooms with a clatter of girls passing through, the landlady barking at them to be quiet, inspecting their beaux before a date. Lizzie found work in a luncheonette, smiling at customers for coins, her hairnet and nails examined before every shift.

Two years turned to three.

One by one the girls left to be married and Lizzie's legs weren't fit for running around a restaurant anymore. She'd saved up a nice sum, booked her passage and was all set to sail when the telegram came. Dada dead. She'd have paid for more words. Did he suffer much? Ask for her? Was he singing right up to the end? She sent home her savings and settled for service again.

Two years turned to ten. Twenty. Thirty.

Mama passed away.

No word from Honora or Kate.

She'd sit in the half light of her maid's room sometimes, look out at the skyline and turn her thoughts to the life she might have lived. See herself skipping down the lane, mayflowers in bloom, Ned waiting by the door, the tea drawn.

She's near the bridge now, breathless, Bootagh Bridge, where she and Maire the Glen would meet of an afternoon after school. Talk about the things they were going to do, the great twists and turns their lives were going to take. Not for them the life of a poor farmer's wife, the cooking and cleaning, the drudgery of housework. No, it was the city they wanted, the shops, the style, the romance. New York, London beckoned. Even Derry would've done.

Maire got no further than a few fields and found not just one husband, but another after he died. Lizzie hadn't heard anything of her in years.

She winds around and around with the road, over the bridge and down again, and comes to a stone wall. Beyond is their house, the roof gone, a sycamore tree taken roots in the kitchen, mountain ash strewn across the floor. Not a sign of life, not the yelp of an animal, the cry of a child, not even the stream is rippling.

She sits on a rock beside the gate. Closes her eyes and sees Mama at the basin, Dada yonder in a field, Honora and Kate running about the yard. She folds into her lap and cries. Long, mournful cries that echo the valley.

She cries for Mama and Dada long gone, for Honora and Kate she knows not where, for her Lady, the girls in the boarding-house, even the bag of cats landlady. She cries for Peggy and the harm Mikey done her. For all the years she's missed here. For Ned and the chance they might have had, for Maire the Glen who went nowhere. She cries for things she didn't even know she was sorry for.

All those days and nights in New York washing and scrubbing, waiting on tables, toiling in other people's homes, never making one of her own. Two years, two years, two years. Why had she stayed so long?

"Eilis, Eilis, is it yourself?" She hardly recognizes her childhood name. "Eilis, Eilis," she hears again, but daren't look. Someone touches her arm. She shudders. "It's me, Maire."

Lizzie wipes her eyes with the sleeve of her stylish new coat. There's Maire the Glen, worn and weather-beaten, face raw, a nest of hair smacked on top of her head, clothes black and heavy of a summer's evening.

"Maire," she says, falling into her friend's arms, where she stays until her sobbing is spent.

"Come," says Maire, taking her by the hand and leading her through the fields. Lizzie has a question that wants askin', but Maire keeps whispering 'whisht.' In the cottage, a man sits beside the hearth, tipping his cap when he sees her, the seat still warm from the heat of him when they lower her into it.

"Tell me something," she says, when the tea is done and the fire about to quench, the light outside dimming. "Is it the meek that inherit the earth?"

"Och, no," says Maire, looking at Ned. "Sure why would we want to? Haven't we all we need here?"

And there they sit, the three of them, the ticking of the clock no longer a lonely thing and ne'er a mention made of the wailing cries that had pierced the valley when Eilis Doherty came back to Bootagh.

Ireland's Own September 2014

WHATEVER HAPPENS

"You'll love it," says Shazz.

"I will?"

"Yeah, and we'll have a laugh."

"Will we?"

"Yeah, so c'mon, you can stay here. Dee won't mind."

"Who's Dee?"

"My roommate. She's in the Bank too."

"Roommate? Oh, I'll have to think about it."

"You think too much already. Oh! And Jan . . ."

"Yeah?"

"Bring some Cadbury's chocolate and Sure deodorant with ya."

"Sure? Don't they have it over there?"

"They do, but it's brutal, OK?"

"OK"

Jan sinks into the red velour seat of the telephone table and rests her head against the wall. She looks at the letter, The World Bank stamped across the top, *we are pleased to inform you*. Shazz had produced the application forms in in Begnet's one day and Jan had filled out hers with coffee cup rings spiralling down the pages. Shazz had been accepted straight away and next thing they're at her going-away party. All they seem to do in the Club these days is say goodbye. And although they hadn't been friends that long, she'd missed Shazz after she'd gone. Six months later, this letter arrives

"September 18th," she tells the man in Global Travel when he asks for a return date. She'll try it for the summer and then it's back to her permanent pensionable in the Department. They'd been encouraging unpaid leave and now they were cutting back on the cut-backs. Three months they'd given her; so this could be her last chance in a way, her final fling, so to speak.

"It's only for the summer," she says when her mother tries to kiss her good-bye. Mam had hardly ever kissed her before.

Only once that she could remember and that was on her First Holy Communion Day, when it had kinda caught her on the nose as she turned away.

It's the same with Rina when she drops her off at the train station. She tries to kiss her too. Jan has known her since she was seven and she's never kissed her either, not even a hug or an affectionate peck.

"Keep an eye on Bren for me?" Jan hesitates before opening the car door.

"Pretend he's dead." Rina grabs the gear stick. "And move on."

"Should I wear a black arm-band?"

"Don't be so smart," Rina says. "Remember, he's my friend too."

Jan stands at the kerb, her rucksack at her feet, her stomach churning, until the Kelly green Mini Minor disappears down Crofton Road. *But, I was your friend first.*

At Dulles Airport, a shuttle bus takes her from the plane to the Arrivals gate where she's led into a massive hallway of glittering glass and chrome. Cinnamon, she decides the smell is, as people surge towards her with wide grins and luminous shirts. An immigration officer stamps her passport and smiles, "have a nice day." Have a nice life, Jan mutters. "You got it," he says. She hoists her rucksack onto her back and steps through sliding doors, slam into a wall of heat. Stopping for a second to catch her breath, the sweat pumping out of her, she looks around for a taxi rank.

"Your first time in DC?" asks the driver.

"Yes." Her heart is too heavy for all this talking. She'd prefer to be back home, heading down to Begnet's, slipping in beside Bren at the bar.

"I'll take you around a few of the sights then," he says.

She didn't realize there were so many monuments, flooded with light and gleaming all around her. "This is the back view," the driver explains, slowing down to give her a better look of the White House.

"Can we go to The Dubliner now?" She wishes she was meeting the girls at home and not in a pub, wishes she could get settled and change out of her peach cotton Capris and crochet top, which are now limp and wrinkled looking.

"Sure," he says, gaining speed again. "So, how are things in Ireland?"

"Grand."

"Don't you have a War over there?"

"Not really."

"Aren't there bombings and stuff?"

"Well, not where I am, it's in another part."

"But it's not that big a country, right?"

"I suppose," she says. "We did have a few bombs, but that was a while ago."

"Gee, you're so cool about it all."

"Sorry," she says. "I'm just tired. Where are you from anyhow?"

"Cambodia," he says, disgorging her onto a steamy sidewalk. By the time she reaches the broad brown door of The Dubliner, she's in a ball of sweat. For feck's sake. She pushes it open. Cambodia?

"Gimme five." Shazz is waving at her. "You're supposed to hit me back, ya thick. You're supposed to say High Five."

Jan smacks her hand, as she gazes around the circular bar with its shiny glasses and brass accessories. She grabs the nearest barstool, expecting to sit in beside Norm or Cliff from *Cheers*. "You look so American," is what she says.

"Feck off," says Shazz who used to wear Michael Mortell suits on a night out. Who would never have had her blonde highlights scrunched up in a pony-tail, wouldn't have been caught dead in a baseball cap and a sloppy top that says *Virginia is for Lovers*. "This is Dee," she introduces a thin, freckled girl, her cap back to front.

"Hi," she says. "What are ya havin'?"

"C'mere Nick," shouts Shazz. "And get my friend Jan a drink."

"A Bud," she says to the lanky barman, the only American beer she knows.

"On me, pet." He knocks on the mahogany counter and hands her a bottle. "Pay me when you're working." An Irish Nick alright, but with a black moustache and tight curls. He looks more like the taxi driver.

"OK," she says, wishing now she'd put on some make-up, dampened down her fringe, wiped the shine off her face. Act mysterious, Rina would say. A sure man magnet she remembers, as Nick pulls away.

"Cute, eh?" Shazz whispers.

"He's grand," says Jan.

She can hear an animated TV commentator, a wall of football machines, the whirring of ceiling fans, cries of 'alright', someone singing *The Fields of Athenry*. She can smell fresh beer and cigarette smoke.

"Let's do shots," says Dee. "Let's celebrate."

"OK," says Jan, even though she'd prefer a cup of tea and a bath.

"Did ya bring the Sure?"

"Oh, no." She can see the cans of deodorant and bars of chocolate stuffed under her seat on the plane, along with six glossy orange packets of Tayto crisps.

"I do have a newspaper though." She's about to fish an *Irish Independent* out of her rucksack when Nick sets down three miniature glasses of coffee liqueur topped with swirls of whipped cream.

"Hands behind your backs," Dee orders. "Bend over and grab with your lips."

Jan grasps the glass and lifts her head up, but the creamy liqueur catches in her windpipe, her eyes fill with tears and her cheeks near burst. She's sure she's going to choke when someone slaps her back and the glass shoots out, hitting the floor in pieces.

"Jesus!" she says and starts to cough; Shazz and Dee double over laughing.

"Not used to it, eh girl?" Nick's eyes are green with tiny flecks of amber.

"Em, no," she says, her face burning.

In the bathroom, she wipes the ring of cream from around her mouth and daubs on the lipstick. *What possessed me to come here?* She smooths the Capris down over her hips and straightens her lacy top. Scraping her mousy brown hair behind her ears, the colour of a mouse's balls Bren would say, she leans into the mirror. Bren had told her she was beautiful once, and she'd believed him. She looks herself in the eye. *There's nothing you can do about any of it now. You're stuck here for the next three months, so you may as well make the most of it. Lose some weight, make some money, and when you get back, you'll be a new woman. And he'll be there, waiting for you.* She splashes water on her face, sucks in her stomach, throws back the head and returns to her seat. She's dying for a real chat like they'd have in a pub at home, but the girls are still sashaying around and around the bar, conversing with every stray cat they can commandeer. Neither of them had even glanced at the *Independent*.

They'd be piling into Begnet's at home, as soon as Glenroe is over. Then down to Peekers, maybe, if the craic is good. Bren would be there, Rina too. She shivers. Nick is whizzing up and down behind the bar, his back muscles rippling through the cloth of his crisp cotton shirt. He catches her eye and winks.

"Better now pet?"

"Yeah."

"How d'ya know Shazz?" His elbows are on the counter, his tea leaf eyes on her.

"Through the Club. St. Begnet's GAA Club."

"So you're a camogie player too?"

"Oh! No." Jan laughs remembering her one attempt with the team, when she'd spent the whole time running away from the ball. "Badminton is more my game. Safer, if you know what I mean."

"I hear ya," says Nick. "Those camogie women can be a rough lot."

"Don't let Shazz hear that or she'll kill you."

"She's killing me already, girl." He straightens up. "So, I suppose you're lookin' for a man too?"

"Em, no, not really."

"You're in the right place anyhow. The money is good and the craic and isn't it better than sitting on your ass at home waiting for the dole to open?"

She's never been on the dole in her life and as for sitting on an ass?

Give us a fag." Dee is back. "And don't break my chops," she says to Nick, plucking a cigarette out of his packet. "I'll buy some in a minute, OK?

Nick sails away blowing a kiss. "Me, break your chops?"

"You're all talkin' like Americans," Jan says.

"You will too," says Dee. "In the meantime, keep your beady eyes off Nick." And with that, she's gone again.

Jaysus!

A band starts playing in an adjoining room, a collection of baseball caps wander in, the jukebox cranks up *Like a Virgin* and Shazz is trying to kiss this lad, but keeps missing his lips. Jan smiles and sways to the music. Every time she empties a bottle of beer, Nick places a full one in front of her. She would love to explain that it's Bren she likes. How she's suspicious of him and Rina. How they're growing away from her and closer together.

"I think Bren likes Rina," she practices saying.

"What's that?" Nick is in front of her again

"A boy I like. I think he likes my friend."

"Fuck him," says Nick

"That's the trouble," she says. "I never did."

He'd been her badminton partner the previous year and they both threw their racquets in the air the night they won their first match. "Don't bend over too far, Janner." He would tease her at the net. "Or I might lose me shuttle in your frilly knickers."

She told him she was mad about him at the end-of-season party, a strip of toilet paper wound around her head in a bandana, her lips purple from all the red wine.

"Oh Janner," was all he said.

"We're still friends?" She'd corralled him the next night at the back of the hall, before the final of the mixed doubles. "Still partners, eh?"

"I'd be more comfortable with Rina," he said. "Because she's not involved. Alright Janner?"

"Alright."

She feels two arms pulling her into an upright position, a straw between her lips, a swirl of soda water gurgling to the back of her throat, Nick whispering, "You don't have to put up with that nonsense."

I don't?

"You have so much going for you," he said.

How would he know?

Shazz sidles up beside them. "Sneaky."

"I'm just telling him about Rina." Jan wriggles away from Nick.

"That's who I mean, there's something sneaky about that one," says Shazz. "You're gonna have a great time here, Jan, d'ya know that? You're gonna have an absolute ball."

Am I?

Jan's face flops forward. Nick is telling her how he's been here five years and is afraid to go home. How he's illegal and might not get back in. How he can't leave his apartment. His furniture. His new video and stereo system. Jan can't imagine not going home because of a stereo. She tries to sit up straight. "When is closing time?"

"Two," he says. "Not able for the pace, eh Janner?"

"I want to go home, that's all. All the way home. I don't want to be here at all." She wrings her hands. "I don't know Shazz that well, for God's sake. And Dee not at all."

"Take it easy," he says. "People come into our lives for a reason, a season, or even a lifetime. It's not that big a deal." He props her up against the back of the stool and she can smell his citrusy cologne, can hear him call, "Shazz, Dee, you gotta get Janner home."

They shepherd her outside, where the air is still heavy with heat, the sidewalk now packed. "Hey, Steve," Shazz waves over a taxi driver. Jan slips into the cold plastic seat of the cab and closes her eyes. *He called me Janner.* The girls slide in each side of her, chatting to Steve. *How do they know the bloomin' driver?* She's aware of cars beeping, sirens, traffic lights and neon. As they career over a wide bridge, the lamp lights force her eyes open; no one here worrying about the electric bill; and she can see the monuments lit up everywhere, even the White House is still glowing in the distance. In front of them is a yellow minivan with a large 'FUCK IRAN' banner flapping from its roof.

"They've got our hostages," Dee explains.

"YOUR hostages?"

"You'll get like that too," Dee sounds defensive. "You'll see."

"But, I'm only here for the summer?"

"That's what they all say," says Dee.

The cab stops outside a tall skinny building. Shazz skips up three steps to the glass entrance, traverses the tiled foyer and kicks Jan's rucksack into a lift.

"Ta Ra," cries Dee outside a door marked 508 that opens into an el-shaped room crammed with two couch beds and a dining-room table. "It's a studio really." Dee hunkers down in front of a fan and flicks open three cans. "Safer that way." She passes one to Jan. There'll be time enough for tea in the morning.

Shazz clicks on the tape recorder and sits cross-legged on the floor. Maura O'Connell's *If You Love Me* bursts into the room. "I'd love someone to sing that at my wedding." She sighs.

"I will if you like." Jan slumps down against the wall. "If I still know you, that is."

"I was nearly married once." Shazz nestles a beer between her thighs. "Goin' out with him seven years I was, since I was seventeen. Let him feel me tits the first night and he said I was a slut. Jokin' of course. Took me to Torremolinos two months later and I thought he was loaded. Thought he was a real man of the world. Until he scarpered off to Saudi. To make money for our future, he said. Then, I met him on

Grafton Street at Christmas with his arm around this one. I can still smell the Bewley's coffee and hear the carol singers outside Switzer's."

Seven years, whereas Jan, what has she except splintered dreams, a loss of hope and a fantasy never fulfilled? Her heart is breaking nonetheless. The pain is the same, for she mourns the loss of what might have been.

"My guy got hurt in a motorcycle accident," says Dee. "When I went into the hospital, found me sister perched beside his bed. Turned out he was seeing her too. Told him I was going to America. The words sorta spewed outa me mouth. He asked if I needed money and I said I did. So, he gave me a blank cheque and I filled it out for five hundred pounds. Haven't looked back since."

"And, are yis over them all by now?" Her eyes are closing, aching for sleep again.

"Of course we are," says Shazz. "There's room in a heart for more than one, ya know."

"And d'yis both fancy Nick?"

"We fancy everyone," says Shazz. "We're lucky like that."

"Like the song says, whatever happens, happens," says Dee. "Don't analyse everything to death."

"But, earlier?" Jan strained her eyes open.

"I was only slaggin', ya eejit," Dee says with a laugh, spots of pink now merging with the freckles on her pixie face. "Just jestin' that's all." She scrunches up her forehead. "So, don't you have a sob story for us?"

"I do, but it can wait." Jan stumbles to her feet. A season, a reason, a lifetime. Can that also apply to love, leaving home, stories and summer flings?

Shazz springs up, Dee presses 'play' and they sing along to the tape, raising their hands at the end for a high five.

"Here's to the summer!" Jan belly flops unto one of the beds, into oblivion.

A condensed version won 2ⁿᵈ place at the Dromineer Literary Festival 2010

MA GRIFFE

Leo stooped by my hatch in the Tech the first day he worked there, his blondish head out of place in the paint-peeling cubbyhole. "What's that book you're reading?" He pointed at the paperback propped against my typewriter. *"Measure for Measure,"* I said, my face burning. "One of the problem plays?" He lifted a brow, his eyes were biro blue.

None of the new teachers acknowledged the receptionist unless they wanted something typed or photocopied. Most men I met thought Shakespeare was a thick.

It wasn't until the Christmas party that I got to sit down in a pub beside him.

His guitar a shield against conversation, I settled for a sing-song instead. A woman should never miss the opportunity to impress, Miss Dolly had impressed on her self-improvement class.

"Magic," said Leo when we harmonized on *Red is the Rose.*

"It was magic," I told my cousin Mags the next day and could feel her eyes roll up to the roof of the telephone kiosk. "Magic me arse," she said. "Did ya shift?"

When he put down his guitar, I held my breath, until I felt his wheaten hair swish against my cheek, whiffed his *Apple Pectin* shampoo. "D'ya want a lift home?" He held out his hand and led me through the hotel lounge, my feet hardly once touching the carpet. I slipped into his silver Ford Pinto; he slid in beside me, his knuckles brushing my knee every time he grabbed the gear stick. From the top of Marine Road, I looked across Dublin Bay at Howth Head. It was hard to know where the starry sky ended and the landscape began.

I tried to act as if I was used to being in a confined space with a man I liked. Tried not to smoke, to disguise the shake in my voice, to pronounce my 'ths', to come across carefree and confident. Confidence is an aphrodisiac, Mags was always saying. I tried to concentrate on what I was saying, on what he was saying.

"You should get yourself a Degree," he was saying, as we rounded the Sallynoggin roundabout. "You don't want to be a two-bit typist all your life?"

A shame, said Sr. Bernadine when I opted for a Commercial Course, and I a scholarship student. A shame, said my mother, and I her brightest child. "We always thought you'd be someone," Dad was wont to add.

"Well you're not a lump of shite." Mags consoled me.

I was grappling for my bag on the floor when Leo stopped the car, tugged at my arm, pulled me towards him, his face illuminated by the street lamp outside my door, his lips finally on mine. I savoured the moment before a kiss begins; the wanting of it sweeter than its taste, its promise. And when his mouth filled mine, I arched into him, giddy with the thinking that we'd always be like this. Girlfriend, boyfriend, an item. Sure I had the wedding dress and all picked out in me head, I imagined telling Mags.

"Go easy," he said, our tongues still, jaws mashed together, eyelashes knitted. He hesitated, pulled away and buried his face in his hands.

"Can I have your number," he said after a sigh, popping a pen from his pocket, writing it down as fast as I reeled it off, my name beside it, big and bold and clear. My name like neon on a torn brown envelope lay on the dashboard of Leo's car. And I had to be content with that.

And with the weddings, dinner dances and parties. When his friends wondered why we only met at formal occasions, I told them I was with an escort agency and Leo always looked for me. "God, you must be good," they said.

Some of these nights ended in kisses, some did not.

In between, his withdrawal left me floundering for air, for space, for my place in the world. Like a parachute jumper searching for solid ground, I enrolled for a night Degree, sometimes suggesting a walk after work or a pint between lectures.

We arranged to meet outside the Pavilion once. He was sitting on the cinema wall when I got there and teased me for being late. A sure sign, said Mags. He took a bite out of my Granny Smith apple and I felt like Eve that day. It was the middle of my Second Year exams and I was dressed in pink. Blouse, skirt, espadrilles and peace earrings, all pink. That was before I went to Color Me Beautiful and they told me pink wasn't my colour; that I was an autumn and should only wear green and brown and rust.

We walked along the East Pier as far as the lighthouse, sat on the rocks and watched the lobster pots dipping in and out of lace-edged waves.

"I can hear your heart beat," I murmured into his cotton shirt.

"It would be worse if you couldn't," he said.

I'd first heard the word unrequited in Leaving Cert English, when we were reading Yeats's poems that had him pining for Maud Gonne. When Miss Horgan with the blue rinse and rouge cheeks would remark, 'You can't make a silk purse out of a sow's ear' every time I took my place in the Honours section. When I failed to get the result and had to shelve the notion of becoming a teacher until later. Until I met Leo.

"He won't marry you now," Principal Doogan said when I requested a career break to study for the Higher Diploma. "Men don't marry brainy women, you know."

I know.

We celebrated my finals in The Kathmandu on Dalkey Avenue. "Miss Kane was right," said Leo raising his glass of white zinfandel before we tucked into the *tandoori* chicken. "You have far more brains than I have, far more brains."

At graduation, the Dean announced that only eleven percent of us would find full-time teaching. He made us look at the person to the left and right, commit their faces to memory, he said, because they'd be immigrating. And so might you, he pointed to people in the amphitheatre at random, you and you and you, he kept indicating. In cycles of thirty years Ireland is drained of its people, he told us, the twenties, fifties and now the eighties. When they're gone, the rest of us may as well turn out the lights. He looked straight at me.

"I'm going to America," said Mags.

"Why?" I was huddled into the telephone kiosk at the bottom of Barnhill Road, hugging my coat, the dog on a lead outside the door, a packet of purple Silk Cut in my fist. "You have a job," I reminded her.

"Ever hear of the word, ad-ven-ture?" she said. "I could do with some, and so could you."

"Oh, I know, but I can't . . ." I couldn't consider leaving, like the fifty thousand that had gone before me that year, despite the Dean's dark words. And even though life without Mags was hard to picture, well . . .

"You're doomed to a life of typing then? Is that all you're good for?"

"Touché," I said. "But, I can't. I can't leave Leo. Even though sometimes I feel like I'm number twenty on his list."

"That's because the first nineteen are himself," said Mags.

I never knew where I stood with him and here I was standing right beside him at another Christmas party. A lone balloon drifted across the dance floor. Miss Dolly was swaying to Slade, her tights wrapped around her neck, Principal Doogan sipping fruit punch *poitín* from a soup ladle, Miss Kane spraying the male teachers with her new bottle of Ma Griffe.

"I have something to tell you," said Leo, his grin lopsided. "Meet me over the holidays?"

"Tell me now," I said, my gaze level with his heart, his green quilted jacket. He should wear blue to match his eyes, but a woman would sort that. "We'll go somewhere quiet," I said, clutching my clutch bag and dashing towards the door.

We drove up Killiney Hill in silence, the rain beating against the windscreen, the wipers tapping out my thoughts. Was he impotent? Infertile? Sterile? He'd had the mumps as a child, so that was a possibility. A child, that was it, he had a child. A woman? Had he met someone else? Was he sick? Dying? About to declare his undying love for me? Say he was sorry for all the times he'd been a cad, cruel, inconsiderate and unkind?

"I'm gay," he said.

Gay?

Like Rock Hudson? And those Englishmen Mags and I met in Mykonos? Who wore mauve dungarees and wondered how we managed our frizzy bits?

"Are you sure?" I wanted to say I didn't mind, didn't disapprove, didn't think any the less of him. But, I couldn't find the words. Nor could I locate tissues, cigarettes or a lipstick, rummaging around my cerise pink bag.

"I've known since I was fourteen." His voice was monotone. "Since boarding school when the Brothers draped my sheet over the dormitory door every time I wet the bed. When I didn't watch *Top of the Pops* with the same thrill as my classmates. When I found myself looking at them instead of Legs & Co."

The lights on Howth Head speckled the black sheet of sky. Raindrops dimpled the windshield. A dog barked behind the obelisk and bushes swayed at the foot of the Druid's Chair. It was said that if you hopped around the stone seat three times on one leg, you'd meet the man you were going to marry within a year. Last time I'd done it, I was ten.

I could see the house I grew up in, the Tech, the Church spire, the piers East and West like two arms embracing the harbour. Mags and I were up here the day the Church went on fire and the smoke filled the sky, obliterating Howth for the first time from our view, racing towards us in clumps of black cloud.

"It's not the end of the world," Leo was saying. "I met a man called Danny and we've been exploring the scene. We made a pact to tell one person over Christmas and I chose you."

"Don't tell anyone else," I said, grasping the sleeve of his jacket. "We'll act like an item, a real couple . . ." I dug my nails into its padding.

"I can't pretend anymore," he said, plucking my fingers one by one from his arm.

The party would be winding down, the band singing *Merry Christmas Everybody,* Miss Dolly slow-dancing with Principal Doogan, the tights now lassoed around his neck, Miss Kane nursing her empty perfume bottle.

"What's with the Ma Griffe?" I had asked her once.

"It means my clutches," she said. "I always wanted to have a man in my clutches." The spongy skin at her throat had quivered. "Tell Leo how you feel," she whispered, her cheeks clenched. "Don't waste any more time. Don't end up like me."

The ground squelched under my feet when I stepped out of the car, the car I had sought every day for three years, in and out the school gates.

"You should have told me at the very beginning," I said. "Or you should never have told me at all." I banged the door shut.

Turning on my pink heels, I walked down the hill towards the telephone kiosk.

Shortlisted for RTE Guide/Penguin award 2013

Diamond Days

Meg was the morning grouch. She never felt like talking until she was up at least an hour. She would lie for a while in that big empty bedroom and listen to the strange sounds outside her window. Strange voices greeted each other with strange accents. Strange music blared from boomboxes outside the Bodega. Strange cars and trucks screeched up and down the street below. Strange languages. Strange people. All strange, but now so familiar.

Inside the girls would begin to stir. Kay was always up first and singing; Val could be heard prancing down the hall, muttering. The kettle would be switched on, curtains drawn and the only tape they possessed soon wafting from the tape-recorder. Mary Black's words of love, heartache and immigration would float through the apartment and Jan would whisper a prayer of thanks to whoever had brought her here. The songs of leaving the land and scenes depicted on Ellis Island were not even faintly reminiscent of the girls' experiences. Sure they missed home, but they could be back there in a matter of hours and pick up the phone whenever they wanted. Plus, they had built another home founded on love and friendship and had formed a bond that would prove impossible to break.

Soon, Trish would arrive in from night duty and keep them amused with anecdotes from her nurse's aide assignments throughout the New York metropolis. In between jumping in and out of the shower, taking turns with the hairdryer, fighting over the mirror and gulping down cups of tea, they would listen to her exploits with the aged and infirm. The note left on the fridge by one young couple was met with stunned silence. *Gone to a movie. If Mom should expire before we return, please call.*

"You'd think she was a tin of peas." Kay snorted.

Her encounter with the poor old man who tried to grab her chest sent them into stitches. He had offered her a hundred dollars by way of an apology, but Trish refused.

"Are ya mad?" cried Val. "We could have put it towards a telly. A hundred dollars for those little things?" She looked at Trish in disgust. "If it had been me, we could've furnished the apartment."

"The whole building, ya mean," said Kay, ducking a slap.

Sometimes, they spent so long chatting, there would be a mad dash for the bus. The heat nearly killed them that first summer. Meg couldn't get used to the fact that after a couple of minutes out of the shower, she would start to perspire again.

They'd have to fight for a seat in the shade outside Woolworth's. Imagine wanting to sit in the shade when the sun was shining? That would never happen at home where they made the most of every minute of sunshine. Sixty degrees was considered a heat wave and would find the whole family out in the back garden in their swimsuits, her father trying to mow the lawn around the blankets and rugs they had spread out on the grass.

At least the Bnx9 bus and the Number 1 subway was air conditioned. Meg couldn't say the same for the apartment. There was only the one fan plonked in the middle of the living-room. At night, they would sit around in their T-shirts and knickers vying for its attention singing along with Mary Black's *Diamond Days*.

"A diamond day," Val would sigh. "Me mother always used to say, today is a diamond day."

At around half past four one morning, the telephone started to shrill in the kitchen and Meg leapt from her bed. Home, she thought, something must've happened at home. She yanked the yellow receiver from the wall. "Help, help," she heard. What the . . . ?

"Who is it?" she asked.

"I lost Mrs. Polansky," the voice said. "Please help me."

"Mrs. who?"

"Oh, God, please help me. What will I do if she's been kidnapped? Killed?"

"Sorry?" said Meg.

"What's wrong?" Kay was beside her, her hands wringing the ends of her tee-shirt into a knot.

"I don't know," said Meg. "Something about a Mrs. Polowsky being dead."

"Mrs. Polansky is dead?" Kay shrieked. "That's Trish's case." Meg could hear a girl screaming.

"Trish, Trish, is that you?" she asked.

"Of course it's me," the voice sobbed. "Who d'ya think it is, ya gobshite. I've lost my client. You've gotta to help me find her before the day nurse comes on."

Oh! God! "OK, ok, give me the address and we'll be there in a jiffy."

"I'll make some tea," said Kay. "You go wake Val."

"There's no time for tea." Meg rushed down the hall. "Ring a taxi. And ask for Ali." She roared back at her, as she untangled Val from her sheet, spinning her half way out of the bed. "Get up. Get up," she said. "Mrs. Polowsky is missing."

"Who?"

Meg didn't answer, but made for her own bedroom, pulled on a pair of shorts and tore back to Val again, who was by now standing naked in the middle of the room, still rubbing the sleep out of her eyes. "We have to go help Trish," she said. "She's lost her client."

The fan was already whirring, the perspiration beating out of her, as Meg sprinted back to the kitchen where Kay was filling three cups with boiling water. "Ali said ten minutes."

"Christ."

Val arrived in, hair tousled, Tee back to front, shorts crumpled, sneakers unlaced, no socks. "What's goin' on? And what has you up so full of beans?" She asked Meg.

"The taxi's here," Kay shouted from the window. "Turn off the fan and I'll put the milk back in the fridge. Val, you put a tape in the tape-recorder."

"For what?"

"For the robbers, of course."

"There aren't any robbers, ya eejit!"

They shoved each other out the door and scuffled down the stairs.

"Are yis goin' out?" A female head popped out of 2C.

"Yeah, sorta."

"Sorry I can't join yis, but Sil's on the graveyard shift. I'd better wait for him."

"Yeah. See ya."

The cab raced up the Deegan Expressway, Ali's hair a black curtain that brushed against Meg's face every time he swung around a corner. She liked the silky feel to it, the scent of his spicy cigarette smoke. "You girls," he kept nodding his head. "What you do now?"

Paddy from the Pinewood said to watch out for him; that he might be a terrorist. He was walking with a limp there for a while, some soccer injury, Ali said. My hat, said Paddy, probably shot himself in the foot during skirmishes. Meg took no notice of that kind of talk.

Traffic was scarce, yet there were people waiting at a bus stop as they turned onto Yonkers Avenue. After the Raceway, they took a sharp right onto a tree lined cul-de-sac, where the houses were painted cerise, turquoise, lime and lemon sherbet, like a child's bag of sweets, Dolly Mixtures, nestled together in the early morning light. They came upon Trish outside a sea-green gate, her face white with fright.

"What am I going to do?" She sobbed when she saw them. "Say if I'm deported?"

"Deported?" said Val. "I'm outa here."

"Me too," said Ali, swerving the cab into a U-turn and speeding off, Val rocking from side to side in the back seat.

"Aren't you a citizen?" Meg looked at Trish. "Weren't you conceived in Chicago?"

"I know, I know," Trish was crying. "But, I could be arrested, right?"

"Let's take it easy," said Kay. "What exactly happened?"

"As soon as I had Mrs. Polansky settled, I fell asleep in the chair. Only for a few minutes mind."

"A few minutes?"

"Well, maybe half an hour."

"Ah Jaysus! Half an hour?"

"And when I woke up, she was gone. The front door wide open and the gate."

"We'll have to call the cops," said Kay, switching into American mode.

"Oh, no, I'll lose me job," said Trish. "Be arrested. Sent home."

"Trish!" Kay roared at her. "We have to find that poor woman, or we'll all end up in jail."

"You're right, you're right," said Trish, clenching and unclenching her fists. "Let's go inside and think about what to do."

They stumbled up the path towards the house. Meg wasn't ready to go home either, she'd only got here for God's sake. What about her job in The Short Stop? The craic with Perfecto the cook, 'you marry me Mama?' He said he'd make her the best waitress in town. Always keep supplies in her pocket was his first lesson. That worked fine until she handed this guy a Tampax with his Diet Coke. Her apron bulging every day with dollar bills. Built-in friends to party with at weekends. The minute they walked into The Pinewood the atmosphere hitting them. The place packed. Clinking glasses. Jukebox blaring. Everyone delighted to see them. The buybacks and backups. No sticking to a round like at home. And of course, the shots.

On her first five consecutive Saturday mornings, Meg was hangin' from the drink. Perfecto suggested hot tea, ginger ale, milkshake and something called bitters to add to her flat Seven-Up.

"You drinkin' those cocktails through a straw?" he asked on one of those mornings and she looked at him peculiar thinking it was because of the Tampax. "Makes the alcohol go straight to your head," he said. "No more straws." She nodded into the toilet bowl. "And no more shots."

They took the steps up to Mrs. Polansky's porch. Meg had dreamt about living in a house like this someday, when she'd saved up the money, imagined herself swaying to and fro on one of these wicker chairs, reading a book. This is what she was aiming for serving all those eggs in the Short Stop.

She saw something rustle in the rosebushes, a flash of pink, heard a repetitive clicking sound. She retreated down the steps. Hissed at the girls to follow. Gestured towards the hedge that lined the garden. There they found Mrs. Polansky in her robe, her feet bare, her head hunched over her knees and her white hair falling out of its rubber band, straggling over her shoulders. "I'm looking for Minnie," she said, her eyes skittering about the bushes.

"Minnie?" Meg hunkered down and took the old lady's ice cold hand.

"My dog," the woman started to whimper. "My lovely, little dog."

Trish shrugged. "There's no dog," she whispered. "She's off with the pixies."

"I'll have a look for Minnie," Meg said to Mrs. Polansky. "Trish will take you inside. Everything will be just fine."

The sun was nudging the sky scarlet and a kind of gold, as Kay and Trish escorted the woman into her house. Meg remembered the note pinned to a fridge in another such household. Nobody had ever reckoned on Mom disappearing or away with the fairies. Meg wished that just once Trish had called Mrs.Polansky her patient; her companion; wished she was more concerned for her employer's plight than she was for her own.

Meg sat on the steps until the gate clicked open and a young girl walked up the path towards her. "Everything OK?" she asked.

"Everything is grand," said Meg.

"Where's Joanna?"

"Joanna?"

"Oh, there she is," said the girl looking at the door where Trish had appeared, shaking her head no at Meg.

Joanna?

"How was your night?" said the girl.

"Not a bother," said Trish. "She's fast asleep, nothing unusual to report."

"Great," said the girl. "See you tomorrow then?"

"See ya," said Trish, hurrying down the path and waving at a cab.

"But, I thought?" said Meg. "Who's Joanna?"

"I'm sorry," said Trish. "It's my sister who was born here. I'm using her social security number. I'm a qualified nurse and couldn't demand the money I'm getting unless I was legal."

They took the cab straight to the Short Stop. Meg wasn't due on 'til ten, but they could all do with a cup of Perfecto's coffee. "I'd murder a plate of greasy bacon and eggs too," said Kay, jumping out of the cab behind her.

They tip-toed over the bird droppings that were tattooed onto the pavement and the rubbish spilling out of kerbside bins. The air was thick with heat and exhaust fumes, the sidewalk wedged with taxi drivers, bartenders finishing for the night, stragglers on their way home and commuters heading down to the City, the subway screeching in and out of the station. Meg spotted their neighbour, Sil from 2C, being pushed out of the Pinewood by Paddy. So much for the graveyard shift.

"It's the party animals again," he roared. "Don't you girls ever go home?" Meg was about to protest when she spotted Trish from the side of her eye, puking into one of the bins. She pulled the hair off her face and held her friend until she finished. For they were friends after all, more than friends in a way, they were each other's family now.

"Trish the Dish have a bad night?" Paddy bellowed.

"Yeah," said Meg. "Yeah, she sure did."

Everything got back to normal after that. If you could call it normal. I'm not normal and no one around me is normal, Meg's Dad used to say. They had visitors at the end of August. Hangers-on, more like. Kay's sister's sister-in-law landed on the doorstep with four others in tow; students who'd been working in Wildwood all summer. They camped down in sleeping-bags and stayed a whole week. One of their mothers rang from Kerry one night and Val put her hand over the mouthpiece and roared, "Have we got a Majella here?"

Then, the roach exterminator arrived. Meg opened the door to a roly-poly man, two top teeth resting on his lower lip. "Cockroaches? I don't think so," she told him.

"There's five of them down in the bedroom," Val yelled at her.

When they did go, it was without a goodbye, thank you, box of chocolates, nothing. "Good riddance," sighed Kay, as she banged the door behind them. "No more uninvited guests," she declared and everyone agreed.

Friends and families were always welcome though. Meg would cook a meal; Val mixed the drinks; Kay cleaned the house and Trish? Well, Trish was always tired after night duty, so she entertained everybody with her stories.

"Did I ever tell you about the time this auld lad tried to give me a hundred bucks for a feel of my boobs?"

They snuggled up anytime they were homesick, two apiece in the beds.

"If anyone saw us, they'd think we were lessers."

"They mightn't be far wrong. Give's a kiss."

"G'way from me."

"Rub me back?"

"NO."

"Ah! You're useless. I won't be sleepin' with you again."

"GOOD."

"Don't forget your breast examinations."

"I'd like someone examinin' them right now."

"Anyone we know?"

"Night Kay."

"Night Val."

"Night Trish."

"Night Val."

"Night Meg."

. . . .

"Night Meg."

"Feck off Val."

"Ah! Jaysus! You're no craic at all."

**Southampton College Journal of New Writing,
Long Island University, 1996**

IF BIRDS COULD TALK

When Mona moved in she brought the bird. A white cockatoo called Dolores who fluttered around in a miniature version of the Taj Mahal. Dolores drove Carrie crazy. The sirens and honking horns had not fazed her the way Dolores did. She kept a sweeping brush beside her bed from where she could rattle the cage without stirring from the sheets. Sometimes she lifted her 'Women on the Verge of a Nervous Breakdown' T-shirt and exposed 36DD breasts to the petrified parrot. The rumpus spilled into the adjoining room where I drifted in and out of dreams. Mona, meanwhile, slept through the whole ballyhoo.

Mona was Carrie's cousin whom Tim, the man Carrie nearly married back home, had absconded with to America after a chance meeting on the DART. Carrie and I followed hot on the heel's pursuit. It was the Eighties, after all, and Irish people every day were hopping every day onto that 747. And I would have hopped after Carrie anywhere, even on one leg. We wound our way out to Woodlawn where we rented an attic apartment, worked long hours in a downtown diner and spent our spare time flitting about neighbourhood bars. Saw no sign of Tim.

Mona, meanwhile, turned up in the lobby one autumn afternoon sitting on a suitcase, the Taj Mahal at her toes. Puffs of steam billowed from the basement laundry and the fragrance of soap powder and fabric conditioner mingled with her honeysuckle perfume. Tim's ardour had cooled it seemed and she had nowhere to live. A letter from her mother sought lodgings.

"When hell freezes over." Carrie shred her aunt's note into confetti and stormed towards the stairwell.

Moved by her bruised, waif-like body and the motley of blue and black marks on her face, I helped carry Mona's belongings upstairs. The occupants of the top storey now numbered three. Four, if we counted Dolores.

We spent hours chatting, the bird and I, about my gruelling new teaching position and the students' indifference. How they teased my accent, ignored my instruction and laughed at the way I said tree for three. Dolores tut-tutted. How I found them sprawled across the desks every morning and could have done with a crane to hoist them upright. How they refused to take a test in calculus one day and were of the opinion that before calculators there was no Math. Her eyes fluttered. How I had swapped my summer catering position for a more noble profession, but now found I provided a different sort of service.

Dolores hissed if I sounded indignant and cooed when I needed consolation. The bird's chitchat broke up the silence that descended on the apartment at dusk; that time of day when the afternoon started to wane, from the time school ended until Carrie bounced in from work.

"Does that bird ever stop yakking?" She hurled bag, books, keys and apron at the cage in an effort to end the cockatoo's ceaseless chatter. No wonder Dolores retaliated with a nocturnal squall.

"And where's the other hare-brained hen?" Yellow tufts spiralled out of her Phyllis Diller hairdo. Carrie couldn't forgive Mona for whisking Tim away; nor could she forgive herself for not warning the girl of his volatile ways. *The tart from the dart,* she liked to call her after several shots of Alabama slammers, the grenadine dyeing her fulsome lips an eerie blood red.

Mona, meanwhile, filled our bare rooms with bric-a-brac from Tarrytown thrift stores and introduced us to Doubledays, a fancy looking bistro on Broadway, which we had hitherto only seen from the sidewalk. In a black lycra dress bound about her petite body, she suggested appetizers like mozzarella sticks and potato skins for us to share, knew the correct temperature for the prime rib and what salad dressing we should choose. She spoke with a lilt; answered 'sure' for the affirmative; and informed the waiter 'we're done' when she wanted the plates cleared away.

We finished the meal with an after dinner drink called Sambuca. I swirled the sweet liquorice liqueur around my tongue before taking a sip of dark coffee. When Mona flicked out her credit card and insisted on picking up the check, even Carrie had to confess. "I'd be a tit in a trance with that job of hers."

Mona worked in Mangos, a fashionable restaurant on the Upper East Side that catered to the Mayor, ABC news anchors, and members of the Kennedy clan. She had even waited on Jackie Onassis. "Wonder whose mangos she had to pull to land that little number?"

Before the busy Christmas season, Mona got Carrie a job there. Now, this was way up Carrie's street and a long ride from Hamburger Haven. This was New York as far as Carrie was concerned. She swapped subway tokens for cab fares; laundromat coins for dry-cleaning bills; Macy's one-day sale for designer shopping at Bloomingdales and local bar hopping for midtown nightclubs.

"God Bless America," she stacked her tips into towers that tottered on an ornate occasional table. "It even pays to be thick here."

Thick, thick, that plank of a girl thinks she's thick. Brains, brains, what good were brains in a land where wits were worth more. Trekking down to the South Bronx every day for half the cash the girls were earning, I lugged my snow-booted legs behind me. Paid not to smile until June, and paid pittance for that, I counted the days, instead of dollars, to the next mid-term. Upon my return from Ireland after the Christmas holidays, I found that the triangle had tilted somewhat, leaving me suspended from the underside. Along with Dolores.

I piled up her dish with pellets, changed her water at intervals, bought her toys to tinker with and strummed her tunes on a beaded window screen. I became anxious if I hadn't heard her tweet in a while and worried that she was having a panic attack if I spotted her plucking her feathers, or banging her beak against the cage.

"Probably needs to get laid," Carrie clucked. "Like someone else I know."

"You have to mind the budgie." A half smile prodded Mona's thin lips during one of her rare contributions to conversation.

My heart dropped, leaving me hollow. Leaving a hole through which the breeze blew. Like long ago. Sitting at my suburban bedroom window, I spent my childhood gazing out at Carrie's world, imagining myself at its hub. Watching her trot to and fro with a gaggle of girls, I longed to be part of their babbling, the focus of their repartee. Then I had to vie with Tim for her attention; I could not now compete with Mona.

"I didn't abscond with your boyfriend to Abu Dhabi, Timbuktu, or Trenton," I said. "I wasn't a tart on the dart, the subway, or a reckless yellow cab." I flapped my hands and fled the room.

Even Dolores was still. Her eyes propped open, her beak rigid.

And if birds could talk . . .

"Legs Eleven," she shrieked one January afternoon when the blue New York sky belied its below freezing temperature. The sole witness to Dolores's first words, I wasn't surprised at her choice. How often had she heard them called out in the dark?

Mangos' distinguished bartender had seduced Carrie the first night she worked there. He had apprehended her outside the *Ladies*, she said, and lured her into the stockroom. When he started to undress her, she couldn't resist. All it had taken was a look and in an instant, their bodies coiled around one another in the back room. Before long, they were gyrating and panting against the dusty barrels. It was all over in time for him to look after the next customer, according to Carrie, and for her to take her first order. By the time she'd patted down her uniform and returned to the waitress station, it was as if nothing had happened. I was agog at her account of events, Mona unmoved.

Legs Eleven became an occasional overnight guest of Carrie's, their lovemaking rumbling through the bedroom wall like a train in a tunnel, accompanied by a thunderous hoot from Dolores.

"Give me a ring?" Carrie's goodbyes always carried a hint of a plea.

"There'll be no ring," he was adamant.

"No ring, no ring," Dolores chanted.

"Mind the budgie." Legs Eleven clattered the birdcage before his departure. "Mind the budgie, the budgie." Dolores rapped in the ghetto beat favoured by my students, as he slammed the door on her song. Rubbing shoulders with the glitterati had assumed him a certain celebrated status, it seemed.

Throughout the melee, Mona seldom stirred in the bed next to mine.

One spring night their intercourse was quieter than usual; the sexual sounds more muffled. No train trundled through the wall; no hoot foretold its arrival in the station. Even Dolores was mute. When, at last the bed creaked summonsing his exit, there was no discomfited leave-taking from Legs Eleven, just the soft thud of his footsteps padding down the hall. Why wasn't he staying the night? And wasn't Carrie supposed to be working? I tiptoed towards the *boudoir* on the pretext of feeding the bird and started when I saw Mona stretched across the bed, not having missed her in my room. An ivory sateen sheet was thrown back to expose petite cupped breasts, threads of her brown hair etched the matching pillow. Her enigmatic smile as difficult to interpret in sleep as it was in waking.

"Mona Lisa, Mona Lisa," Dolores chirped, as I slid the door shut. "Legs Eleven loves Mona Lisa."

It was time to hone my pedagogic skills. What better way to while away those long afternoons I had grown to abhor. What better pupil than a parrot.

"Mona Lisa loves Legs Eleven." I taught her to intone.

Carrie's brow crumpled.

"And Legs Eleven loves Mona Lisa." The cockatoo sang on cue.

Carrie twisted her straw locks into corkscrews around her finger.

"Legs Eleven likes the budgie." The bird parroted. "Mona's budgie."

Carrie's round eyes narrowed into icy blue slits.

"Dolores is no daw." She cut short one particular rattling of the birdcage. "He's been here, hasn't he? With her?"

She challenged the two of them at work one day and caused such a furore that Legs Eleven asked her to leave. Manhattan barmen possessed as much sway as the proprietors, Carrie discovered. In a New York minute, she lost her lover and her job. The following morning, Mona announced she was moving out. Heading to the Hamptons, she said, with one of the customers.

"Mind the budgie," Carrie muttered, as we watched her struggle down the stairs with her baggage. Before she alighted into an awaiting cab, the door of the Taj Mahal sprung open and from our attic porthole, we watched Dolores soar into the pungent Bronx air towards Tarrytown.

"I didn't know she could fly." I stared after Dolores until she was a speck in the sky.

"But, you knew she could talk." Carrie peered at me through a tangle of coloured glass beads.

Shortlisted Francis McManus radio award 2011

FRANKIE & JOHNNY

Every Thursday at five, Frankie and I met in Norah O's Tavern on the tip of Long Island and worked side-by-side until ten. While he mixed markdown cocktails and I served half-price hamburger platters, we helped ourselves to Norah's house-blend coffee and we talked bullshit about books.

"Who's your favourite Irish writer?" he asked one night, pumping a shot of Jack Daniels into my end-of-shift decaf.

"Oscar Wilde," I said, straddling a barstool.

"How about that?" he said. "With all your books, your Degrees, I'd a taken you for a Joyce or a Beckett."

Throughout that summer, my first on the North Shore, Norah always scheduled Frankie and me on her two-for-one dinner shift. Because we were her best team, she said, and we were both Irish. His folks had arrived over around the time of the Mayflower; my Mom sailed up the Hudson on the Saxonia. As well as lessons in literature, I taught him curse words and cockney terms I had learnt from my real deal West Clare cousins. His favourite was 'bag of coal'; the East London slang for sex.

"Because coal keeps you warm, right Joni?"

"Em. Not exactly," I said, slowly rotating on the swivel stool. "Coal rhymes with hole . . . as in, did you get your?"

"Get your hole?" He raised a bleached brow.

"Get laid," I said, spinning.

Frankie was a surfer, craggy and weather-beaten in a Mick Jagger sort of way, although a lot prettier with his sea blue eyes and sun streaked hair. He even claimed to have met the Stones when they came to town in the seventies and stayed next door to him in the Memory Motel.

I had packed in a bookkeeping post in Pelham and was on a summer hiatus. That should give me enough time, I thought. Enough time to get used to the fact that Mom was finally gone for good. Enough time to decide what to do next. Sinking into the sand every day, marinating in coconut oil, my skin and hair crisp, I hardly noticed the waves.

"You've been to the beach," Frankie would shake his head in disbelief. "And you didn't see the Ocean?"

"You got it," I'd say, reckoning I'd never be as cool as his Sixties chicks.

Frankie knew them all – Peter Beard, Andy Warhol, Marianne Faithful, even Bianca, back about twenty years or more. My first brush with celebrity was with Paul Simon in the Naturally Good health-food store where I was sitting on a sack of sweet potatoes eating a choc-ice. He asked where I had found the cacao covered ice-cream bar and I had to lean out of his way while he slid open the freezer door.

"Literary chick charms songwriter," Frankie teased me that Thursday, five weeks into our friendship. "Right, Joni?"

"Sounds good to me," I said.

Waitress woos bartender would be better. Makes him her tart. Treacle tart. Sweetheart.

Norah started singing *Frankie and Johnny were lovers.* By the time she got to *he was her man, but he was doin' her wrong,* I was ready to hop her peroxide head off the counter.

"Well, you're both unattached." She sipped her nightly *rosé* through a straw. "And already sort of entwined in a song. But, your sell-by dates are about to expire." She sucked the final pink dregs of her drink and slammed down the glass. "Ya gotta strike when the iron is hot."

Frankie struck straight away by bringing me back to his rented room. Perched on the solitary chair, I clutched a black patent purse on my lap, matching heels tucked under the seat, everything else strewn on the floor, including my host. Newspapers, books, coffee cups, utensils, cassette tapes and recorder, even the mattress was at ground level, from where he passed me a joint.

Smoke swirled to my brain; stung my ears, eyeballs, nostrils, nose; blazing a trail down my windpipe, detonating in my lungs. Leaping from the chair, I step-danced over the debris, gesturing at Frankie for a drink. I was the only student at Spellman High that had graduated ignorant of the joys of pot and sex, due to Mom's mania for corporal punishment, a passion she had picked up in Industrial School.

"Been smoking that shit since I was sixteen," Frankie said, handing me a beer can. "Met the old man out on his beat one night and had to stuff a bag of weed down the front of my pants. When he asked about the strange bulge between my legs, I said I had spent the night with an up-Island chick and was still stoked." Frankie half shut his eyes. "Dad ushered me home with a clap on the back, his NYPD buddies smacking me high-fives."

There were no tales from my Bronx childhood that I could share with Frankie. No place in the past for us to meet. The present might be another story. My mind started to drift out to sea with the drug. What if Norah was right? What if Frankie and Joni were destined for the end of the island, our heads a tangle with seaweed?

First, I had to find a year-round residence. My summer rental would terminate in September and I was back to a brownstone in Pelham. It was time for Mom's never-known-to-fail Novena. I folded the crumpled prayer card, found on her bedside locker beside an empty medication bottle, into my apron pocket. In between dishing out *Danny Boy* and *Bridget* Burgers, I recited nine Our Fathers, nine Hail Marys and nine Glory Be to Gods, nine times a day for nine days and on the ninth day, I was rewarded with a two-bed duplex in Hither Hills.

"I got it, I got it." I torpedoed into the Tavern waving my apron like a flag.

"Got what?" asked Frankie, a slip of sandy hair brushing his pockmarked cheek. "Your bag of coal?"

That night, he laced my coffee with Tia Maria and tipped an extra shot into my end-of-shift Calypso. I was rattling off the specials sing-song style and flinging out the platters Frisbee fashion. I had finally found somewhere I could consider settling; far from Fordham Road and my suffocating past; far enough away from the world without falling off it altogether.

At the stroke of ten, we tugged down the shades, closed the shutters and switched off the orange neon sign. What better way to end the day than at the roach motel? The local name for his lodgings was lost on me at first, like the bag of coal had been on him. Moving on the makeshift mattress; our bodies curving and arching, limbs flailing, flesh skimming flesh, we partook of both, as the night cloaked the town in darkness.

Thursdays were subsequently spent waiting for a look or a sign that the night would not end with our shift. The other six days, I trailed him to the docks, marinas, surf shacks and harbour bars. And sometimes at night, I sat in my car outside the Memory, staring at Frankie's window.

Meanwhile, he helped move my meagre belongings into the upstairs apartment and stayed through Thanksgiving.

"Can't leave my Celtic chick all alone on the Holiday," he said, arriving that Thursday with a bookcase he'd banged together and some take-away turkey. Sharing an after-dinner Bailey's and homemade hash brownies, we watched the sun set over Fort Pond and delved into *Dorian Grey*.

"That dude Dorian had the right idea." Frankie shot me his schoolboy smile. "Imagine never having to grow old?"

"Beats the alternative," I told him. "And he does die in the end."

"So the moral is?"

"Be careful what you wish for," I said.

While snow cascaded outside my hilltop home, I passed the time knitting an Irish fisherman sweater. Needles clicking, I wove my fantasies into the basket, beehive and diamond design. If we were to get married, it would be said forevermore that we did so late in our lives. Against whose life was such a barometer measured? Following Mom's crinkled pattern, I spun a bridal shirt like an Aran island girl of long ago. During courtship, the story went, she would knit her sweetheart a *gansey* and if he accepted, it signified his affection for her. I even dropped two stitches in the twisted cable and had it all wrapped up for Christmas Eve.

"Something else to keep me warm, eh Joni?" Frankie studied his reflection in the motel window.

"Like love," I said, drawing mock quotation marks in the air. "And, according to Irish folklore, a defect in the pattern helps identify drowned fishermen."

"I ain't going under," he said, the tree lights flicking on and off behind him. "Just up Island. To my family. You're welcome to . . ."

"Nah," I stopped him. "I never liked Christmas anyhow. You're hot to trot then."

And I was on my own. Todd Sloan.

Mom always maintained I was too plain, too comely for a handsome man. And she was right. With two Degrees, but not the right one, she said, without the common sense one, I'd never amount to anything. And I hadn't.

Winter wrapped a shroud around the town, disconnecting its citizens like driftwood. Tourists departed and business diminished. One staff member could have handled the single digit diners, but Norah still scheduled two.

"You're too interesting to be alone," she said and I unravelled.

Following a non-tipper to the door, I snapped at him, 'something wrong with the service?' Finding a dime on another table, I dashed through the dining-room, into the kitchen and out through the parking lot, spinning the coin at the offender's feet.

"Whoa! Joni." Frankie was behind me, holding up his hand. "I thought you were so holy? With all your prayers?"

"And I thought there was something," I said, "when there was nothing."

The clock ticked passed the hour of five one Thursday, the neon light blinked OPEN and lunch menus were replaced by those for dinner. I wrote up the specials board, polished glasses and hung them on their overhead hooks, sliced the whiskey cake for desert and fruit for the cocktails, settled beer in the freezer and kept the ice machine in motion. Jumping back and forth between our two sets of side-work, I clenched Mom's prayer in my apron pocket every time the dining-room door flung open.

"Looks like lover boy's a no-show," Norah said, reaching for a glass of *rosé*.

At ten, I abandoned my post and raced out onto Main Street; traversed the wide thoroughfare where in January we could lie out flat on the ground and not be run over; swung around by Naturally Good and drew to a stop outside the Memory.

The Stones thumped softly inside the open window, as a gust of wind parted the faded nylon curtains. Frankie was sprawled across the mattress, staring at the ceiling, a butt smouldering between his fingers.

"My waitress chick," he said when he saw me. "What's up, Joni?"

"It's Thursday," I told him.

"Thursday?" He sprung up, the ash sprinkling like snow. "Holy shit," he said.

Holy shit. Brad Pitt. Two-bob bit. Tom-tit. Angel's delight. Shite.

Frankie cocked his head. "Kick ass without me tonight, Joni?"

"Ya know somethin'?" I said. "I did."

Waves crashed onto the shore, as I raced towards the beach, my feet squishing the wet sand, Mom whispering, 'the story of your life, Joni, the story of your life.' Norah singing, *this story ain't got no moral, this story ain't got no end.* Frankie enveloping me in his warm woolly sweater, the two slipped-up stitches a beacon, the salt air stinging our lips. Me smiling, 'No Mom that was your life. Your life.'

Longlisted Fish Short Story competition 2010

THE PRINCE OF DARKNESS

He was slouched against the bar, a smirk on his face, cigarette at the side of his mouth. Irish, definitely, but not the sneakers and cut-off jeans, milk-bottle-legs brigade that poured into town every May; who two weeks later were turning their baseball caps back to front and ripping the sleeves out of their soccer shirts. He had the fierce blue eyes alright, the caul of black hair, the fistful of freckles flung across his face, but the tan leather waistcoat and cowboy boots looked out of place in thirty degree temperatures. If he wasn't a J1 student, what was he doing here then?

"Fishing," he said after I nosed up to the counter and squeezed in between himself and Jaffa Cake.

"We're gonna get him on a boat," said Jaffa Cake, bristling with importance, even though he hadn't gone dregging himself in ages. "This here's Pat. Pat Donovan. A friend of mine. So be nice to him, Gem."

I was just back from Woodstock. Not the 1969 mud fest, but its anniversary twenty-five year later, and I had been dying to be nice to a man all weekend.

"What do you think of the POD?" Tess sidled in beside me, petite and feather-light; her hair a halo of curls, copper and shiny, like Jaffa Cake's with conditioner. "Nice, eh Gemma?"

"What's with the 'O'?"

"O?"

"Shouldn't it be PD for Pat Donovan?"

She tipped a beer bottle into her mouth. "P-O-D is for Prince of Darkness."

I'd spot his bicycle outside Ronjo's Saloon, the Bait 'n Tackle, Jake's Liquor Store and the Trailer Park at Ditch. Come upon him cycling around the pond. Beep. Wave. Smile. Drive on. Awful August was upon us, with the population swelling from two to ten thousand and the roads resembling racing tracks. Twelve hours a day. Every day. A driver with Pink Tuna Taxis, I knew where everyone was and with who.

So, when I clocked off at six on Labor Day Monday, I told Cabs to drop me at Ronjo's instead of my usual jaunt home. "Need to wind down," I said. "Celebrate the end of the season."

"I hear ya," said Cabs, even though he didn't. He was already revving up for the next fare, aiming to get there before Holy Mackerel.

The POD was hunched over the counter that evening, the first in September, in a black, Black Eyed Peas tee-shirt and the signature leather waistcoat.

"Where's Jaffa Cake?" I asked, my insides jangling.

"The red lad's got a gig tonight. Gone for a run with the mutt first. Did yis have a rendezvous or something?"

My eyes flicked around the bar, afraid to meet his, for of course I knew that Jaffa Cake was on Gin Beach throwing sticks into the sea for his border collie, Ajax. Knew he was working later at The Windjammer, bar-backing for Tom Cruise and his crew, who had been stashing away four to five hundred bucks a shift all summer. Jaffa Cake was the only man in town who started work in earnest on Labor Day.

"Tess?" I asked, gesturing at Puck for a drink, the same again for the POD. Tess was busy bussing tables at the Ocean Surf, I knew; said she'd meet me later. Said we'd have a right auld session to sign off the summer.

"Nah," he said. "Don't know what she's at."

She'd been catching up with him here and there, I knew, having pints with him. Tess was one of the lads, down to her tight jeans and Timberland boots. Men preferred being with girls who liked being with them.

The sky was roaring red as the sun slipped behind Block Island, the sunset crowd vanishing with it. Puck replaced our drinks; another vodka 'n coke for me, tequila 'n lime juice for the POD. He'd been expelled from boarding school, he was saying, caught nicking cigarettes in the local sweet shop; a bottle of wine from the chaplain's vestry.

He'd met Jaffa Cake in a Brooklyn squat, both at a crossroads. Jaffa Cake had moved further out Long Island and got a job laying bricks on the Rough Riders apartment block; the Killing Fields, he called it. The POD made for San Francisco and worked on Fisherman's Wharf, taking cruise boats back and forth to Sausalito.

"I was on me way home," he said, "when I stopped off here to see the Cake, and the bollocks filled me head with fishing and making wads o' money."

At closing time, he twisted his bicycle into the back seat of Pink Tuna and sat in beside me up front, a wheel between our heads. When Cabs swung onto Edgemere towards Ditch, I said "Pat's comin' along with me." Cabs screeched on the brakes and swerved without a word towards my cottage.

All the times I'd dropped people home, or picked them up in places they didn't normally kip. Now it was my turn.

The POD kissing me, his fingers clutching my hair, his lips pressing mine, the sections of my Ikea couch separating underneath us, him lifting his hip and kicking them together. *Where's the bedroom?* His voice husky; I nodded 'no'; his lips persisted, his tongue sliding in and out of my mouth, his hands like a dancing octopus. *Where's the bedroom?* Well . . . Sure . . . I might as well go for it . . . In with us then to my yellow room with the daffodil duvet. Tess said she never put out until the third date, but how could a girl be sure of that?

The next morning, he was stroking my eyelids with his fingertips. I felt him draw near and kiss them, each one, while I lay there, pretending to sleep.

A man slouching around my cottage, admiring my Celtic crosses and Aynsley china, supping tea and dunking digestive biscuits, his jingly bits jingling. Walking around the pond with me, its waters glistening teal and turquoise; down the hill to Captain's Cove, the seagulls flapping around us, the sky a silky blue, *won't you take me to Funky Town* blaring from the Tipp Motel.

"I'd better start trawlin' some fish soon," he said, one hand securing his leather vest around my shoulder, the other steering the bicycle. "Or I'll have to go."

I crossed my fingers in his waistcoat pocket.

The POD mapped my September days. Cruising in a baby pink station-wagon, up and down to the Docks, along the Old Highway, around the pond, east side and west sides, watching the foliage turn rust, aubergine, magenta, I watched out for him. The summer people departed in droves, most of them in the back seat of my car, and that feeling of being left behind started to seep in. Sitting on a burnt-out beach log, I gazed along miles of sparkly sand as far as the cliffs jutting out onto the horizon. That first summer, walking this strand, the sun scorching my face, the beach grass swaying - the worst place for ticks we were told, I decided to join the other sixty or so who were staying.

Leps, the locals called us, short for Leprechauns. Drifters, they said we were, lacking in ambition; children afraid to grow up. For eight or nine of us, I'd say, it was something more than that.

"Ten," said Tess.

I was on the lookout for a fare one day when I spotted her on a bench outside the Bait 'n Tackle. "I've something to tell you," I yelled through the taxi window.

"I know," she said.

"What d'ya think?"

"We're all a bit desperate this time of year."

"It's not just that . . ."

"If you've found someone to snuggle up to for the winter, go for it."

"I thought maybe you liked him too?"

"Who?"

"The POD."

"The POD? Jaffa Cake said it was him you were snogging."

I had kissed Jaffa Cake once, out on Tess's lime-green deck after Thanksgiving dinner and I full of turkey and chestnut stuffing and Empire State shots of Sambuca.

"Let's do Eiffel Towers," she had suggested earlier, lighting a match to the tiny glasses, sticking her finger in the flame and holding it up like a torch, as she downed the drink and then licked her finger to quench the fire. Jaffa Cake's lips were sticky, his tongue sweet from the liquorice, his kiss full of feeling.

"Empire State," I said when our mouths finally parted.

"Huh?" He looked at me, his hair a cloud of fizzy orange.

"The shot. It was the Empire State, not the Eiffel Tower."

"I thought it was the Statue of Liberty," he said, and we kissed again.

Tess appeared with a doobie then, blowing rings of smoke into the frosty night and I didn't stand a chance.

And every year, we swore we wouldn't stay beyond September 15th and, every year, it got later and later. By the time the POD arrived, I'd clocked up six year-rounds.

"Yis are all running away," he said one November night in Ronjo's, his eyes screwed shut, a butt between his thin lips. The leaves had fallen off the trees and he still didn't have a job. "I wouldn't want to stay anyhow. And I wouldn't want to find love here. Then again," he paused. "I wouldn't mind being surprised."

I nodded my head in agreement, as if I was rooting for a surprise for him too, as if instead of aching, my heart was opening like a bunch of blooming hydrangeas.

The trees started to look like spooky black lines and the landscape a sort of sepia. My customers were reduced to out-of-work fishermen and food stamp fares; Liquor Store deliveries and carting the Leps back and forth to Ronjo's. I cooked Christmas dinner for the few that were left, the pond frozen over and the cottage bathing in a sunset coral.

The POD sat on my daffodil bed the next morning, smoking a cigarette and drinking coffee from a blue, Grecian design, *we're here to serve you,* paper take-out cup.

"I might as well be at nothing here," he said. The Holiday was over as suddenly as it had started and winter upon us again like a blanket. "I have to get out of this ghost of a town," he was saying. "Poxy people slithering in and out of shadows, afraid to catch your eye, afraid to say they're staying because that means there's as bored with themselves as everyone else is." He was prancing naked around the room now. "Why do you stay in such a poxy place?"

"Loneliness is a state of mind," I quoted Tess. "And I have ducks and swans swimming by my window. Deer showing up sometimes in my back yard. The beach in December, the Lighthouse lit up for Santa, the snow stacked outside my screen door. And, all of a sudden, spring breaks through. There's the Parade to look forward to, swims in Hidden Lake, sunsets in Ronjo's, cycles to Lazy Point and next thing the tourists are back and the students. It's summer again," I said. "It's Paradise."

"It's the end of the fucking world," said the POD, pulling on his pants, his chunky pullover and his woollen skull cap. "More like Hell than Heaven. Tis time yis copped on and got back to the real world." He stormed out of the cottage, the screen door swinging rat-ta-tat-tat against the shingle.

"GEMMA PICK UP," he was roaring into my answering machine.

"Yeah, Gem, please." That was Jaffa Cake.

"I'VE MISSED THE BLEEDIN' JITNEY. GONNA MISS THE BLEEDIN' PLANE. GEMMA, PICK UP."

"Gem, please. Puck took my keys, won't let me drive. Tess you tell her . . ." Jaffa Cake again.

"Yeah, Gemma, ya gotta get him to the Airport. Pleeeease?" That was Tess.

"GEMMA, THERE'S A GOOD GIRL. I KNOW YOU'RE THERE AND I KNOW YOU'RE MAD ABOUT ME, SO C'MON, PICK UP, FOR JAY-SUS CHRIST'S SAKE . . ."

I lay there in the dark listening, saw the girl knocking at a door, heard a man's voice *Come in,* her hand turning the doorknob,

There's a good girl, the door creaking closed. And she goes there willingly, no matter how many people say she doesn't.

I played the tape over and pressed delete. Someday you'll meet your Prince, my Gran used to say and I never got the chance to tell her, I already had.

Cabs took the POD to the airport, Tess told me, a two-hundred dollar round-trip fare. She'd been drinking all day with them and he couldn't stand, she said. Jaffa Cake wasn't much better. Why didn't you ring me earlier, I was looking at her thinking. The POD was in Texas by then, laying television cables.

"We're calling him the Cable Man now," said Jaffa Cake, one freezing February morning when I dropped him off at Captain's Cove. There was the promise of work on the Lazy Bones and the Leps were already counting down to Paddy's Day.

"Your hair looks nice," I told him.

"Must be the VO5," he said, pronouncing the letters V O like a word - *voh.*

"Jaffa . . ."

"Yeah?"

"Were ya ever sorry ya stayed?"

"Nah." He shrugged. "Just sometimes sorry I stayed so long, that's all."

I gazed at the icy grey sky, at the sea the same colour. There was no sign of the horizon at all. "See ya so?" I said, as he sprung from the car.

"Yeah, see ya," he said, looking at my lips before closing the door and I sat there a while and watched him amble towards the fishing boats.

August 2014

THE HOTTEST PLACE ON
THE STRETCH

Flo arranged chunks of pineapple on the Pîna Coladas, popped in a parasol and eased a tray onto her shoulder. The beach was bare that day, with splashes of sunlight glinting off the navy blue horizon. Four thousand feet of sparkling sand and not a sinner on it. Lunch was steady at the Fishy Fish House, mainly hikers in from the walking dunes and birdwatchers visiting a nearby observatory. A passing car hooted its horn and diners responded with a wave, or a whistle if their midday cocktails were starting to sink in. A willowy figure sauntered up to the bar, tall and thin and beautiful with a cascade of skinny black braids spiralling down her back.

"Need any help?" she asked, a frill of white teeth sitting on her lips.

"Talk to Clem," Flo said, inclining her head towards the tree stump where he sat chin on chest. There had been a stream of job hunters through the restaurant all week, a familiar sight on the stretch the week before Memorial Day, the week before the season properly began.

She deposited the drinks on a patio table and swung into the kitchen to pick up a calamari platter. Scents of jasmine and rose from the shrubbery mingled with the *marina* and *au poivre* sauces.

"I hated it," she said to the chef

"What's that?" said Kenny.

"Askin' for work. Always felt I was beggin'. Sometimes I'd pretend to use the restroom and dash back out again."

"Didn't bother me," said Kenny, scooping rings of fried squid onto a plastic plate. "They needed the help and I needed the money."

"Wish I was you, Ken." Flo dressed the dish with sprigs of parsley and a slice of lemon.

He took a swig of tequila from a bottle he kept behind the *bain-marie*, leaned forward and placed his other hand on her cheek, two of his fingers stroking her skin from the chin upwards. "And I wish I was you; too smart for this shit."

She grimaced and swiped them away. "Well, Oprah said to follow my bliss, so come September I'm hitting the highway."

"You say that every year," said Kenny.

Clem hurried in, face flushed, silvery pony tail askew, baseball cap skip left.

"Hey Kenny," he said. "See who I just hired. Priscilla's her name. Nice, eh?"

Kenny glanced out the window. "Sure is." He whistled. "She's like, like. I'd like to be the saddle on her bike."

"She's startin' tomorrow." Clem puffed out his chest. "I haven't lost it yet, eh? Still the stud, eh?"

"She'll fit right in," Flo said on her way out, where she met Priscilla peering at the unmarked bathroom doors.

"Either will do," she told her.

He put her waitressing first, to see how she got on, he said. Out back by the truck, an old eighteen-wheeler that doubled as a freezer and storage room, Flo had her hosing slugs off lettuce leaves, shredding cabbage for the coleslaw, slicing lemons and mixing tartar sauce.

"What's next?" she asked, the sweat glistening on her brown forehead.

Next, she had her pinning orders on the line, crying 'pick up' and balancing trays on her hips, hollering 'either will do' and mixing strawberry mango daiquiris. She was trailing Flo across the deck, into the dining-room, out onto the patio. A cup of house red landed on a white linen lap; a purplish onion was served with a vodka martini and mako shark steak brought to a customer who'd ordered sirloin.

"It's a bloody fish house," Clem yelled. "They can't cut steak with a plastic knife, for chrissake. And we've no dishwasher." He spat into the bushes. "Environmental regulations my ass."

He tried her as hostess the following day, to see if she did any better. And although she mixed up the table numbers and forgot who came next on her list, the men were enthralled, the women in awe, as Priscilla swanned around in a cloud of chiffon. Two nights later, she and Clem had supper in Sapore di Mare.

"I don't believe it," said Flo, flaying lettuce leaves for the dinner shift.

"Bucks, babe," said Becky, a girl with two ropes of yellow hair who'd been hired to tend bar. "Money talks and bullshit walks in this business."

"Ya think she's after his money?"

"I think she's found herself a sugar daddy."

Clem looked all of fifty-four that summer and Priscilla, thirty years his junior, had got there just in time. "Twenty-seven," he'd tell the boys at the bar. "I'd never date anyone over twenty-seven."

He'd never date anyone he worked with he'd told Flo, as they lay on the floury sand, his hand under her shirt. "This place is hot." He'd whispered. "And ya know why it's hot? Ya know why it's hot? It's hot because of me."

It had been a tumbledown shack for years - a grey boarded shed on the side of the road where he used to stop for a burger on his way down from Philadelphia. The sort of place you'd see in a Fifties movie with Marilyn Monroe pulling up in a Thunderbird. In 1995, movie stars and baseball players were spotted there, talk-show hosts and soap opera stars. They were even vetted for the Secretary of State.

Clem had ordered the kissing-fish umbrellas; a striped awning; flowers to tumble out of the hanging baskets and terracotta pots; little green lanterns to blink on the bushes. He'd commissioned a neon sea world for the patio, individual fixtures designed and hand-crafted by Mundy Hepburn.

"He's Katherine Hepburn's nephew." Priscilla cajoled the customers. She was soon making so much money, Clem complained it could've been her name above the door.

Still, they came to see him and hear his stories. Like the one about Sitges. "I used to own a whole town in Spain," he'd start, his face getting redder with the telling. It was hard to know if the ruddy complexion was from too much sun, or the beer. Despite the rough exterior, he did call his eighty-five year old mother every morning.

"She asked if the new girl was a bit on the dark side." Clem looked out onto the dunes, his eyes never once meeting Flo's.

"What did you tell her?"

"Mommy, I said, she's as black as the ace of spades."

By the middle of June, people were wandering up the ribbon road from the beach, strolling down from Ocean Avenue motel rooms, driving in along Route 109. Flo flipped over the tables, through lunch and dinner shifts, while Becky churned out frozen fruit cocktails and Priscilla kept the customers in a line.

Clem marched up and down beside them, spindly legs shooting out of khaki shorts, a Marlboro in one hand, a Heineken in the other. "Hi ya hon." He kissed the women's cheeks.

"Hangin' in there." He responded to the man-hugs.

"They all love me," he'd shrug and there'd be a cheer from the boys at the bar.

"I need tables, tables" he hissed at Flo. "Tables, tables," he roared across the deck. "And don't forget to smile." He prodded her. "Smile. Puss. Smile." He jabbed above her waistband with his thumb. "Priscilla said you never fricking smile."

He used to promise he'd make her Manager; put her in charge of schedules and shifts, the bank deposit and wages. Pay her a salary, he said. She could discard the smelly tee-shirts, the sweaty sneakers, the apron stained with fish oil and lobster juice and wear dresses for a change. Six years, she'd waited. Six seasons on the floor, Flo had waited for a real job.

For the Fourth of July weekend, Priscilla's brother, Dane, joined Kenny on the line and a couple of sisters were ferried in as waitresses.

"Are there many more of them?" Becky asked.

"Lots more," he said. "So, you'd better watch your ass behind that bar."

He took to wearing a sarong and saying he was from Kingston. "Bob Marley died in my arms," his mantra.

He'd hire a couple of cabs to transport staff and stray customers to The Calypso Club. Fan out five one-hundred dollar bills on the bar and say, "We'll stay until it's gone."

"Move those hips, Mama Flo." Dane would sway in front of her on the dance floor. "You got lots o' hips."

"Gee thanks," she'd shrug and they'd both flop over laughing.

He grasped her waist one night with his long twig fingers. "Why don't you and I make a Jam-Am baby?" He drew her close.

"Forget about it," she said.

The sun was a plum by the time they'd finished breakfast in Bill's Pancakes, the sky a deep pink over Ocean Avenue. Flo lay in her chalet listening to the rustle of waves and the ripple of parasail wings. She tried to imagine his pillow lips on hers, his white marble eyes searching for her in the dark.

"I'm sorta sorry now," she told Becky the next day.

"No way?" Becky screamed above the blare of the blender.

"Why not?" Flo asked. "He's young. Beautiful. What's not to like? Oprah says love has no boundaries."

"Oprah's a millionaire, she can do what she likes. Trust me, it won't work," said Becky. "Stick to one of your own."

"The last one of my own told me he had a wife and child on Cherry Hill."

"Gosh," said Becky. "You sure pick 'em."

"They pick me," said Flo.

She pressed through the growing crowds, dodged sister waitresses with their trays, elbowed up to the bar for drinks, squeezed into the kitchen to pin-up orders; pick-up orders, weaved through meandering lines for the bathrooms. And all Clem could do was talk about Priscilla. About the credit card bills she was clocking up on hair extensions, deep-sea massages, salt rubs and shopping trips to the Gap and Banana Republic.

"That's what she's used to," he said one day, topping his ash into the nearest terracotta pot.

"Ain't too many spas in Shantytown," Becky said, the words sizzling at the side of her mouth.

"Oh, Becky!" Flo would've laughed, if she wasn't so tired from it all.

The girls were setting up the bar for lunch, the midday sun branding the backs of their necks.

"I thought I was a gonner last night," Clem kept on talking. "I thought I was gonna go like Rockefeller."

Flo gave Becky a questioning look.

"Rockefeller died in the sack," Becky whispered, mopping her face with the tail of her bandana.

Flo stuck two fingers in her mouth and Becky crouched down behind the bar laughing.

"Busy ladies?" Priscilla swept past, her braids rippling like slippery eels.

Then Kenny lacerated the tip of his thumb hacking lobster tails; danced around the *bain-marie* screaming, "I ain't takin' no more orders from no . . . n . . . n . . . nobody;" flung his white coat at Dane and smashed one of the neon fixtures on his way through the dining-room. Just before the biggest month of the year, they lost their head chef.

"I fired men over my shoulders in Vietnam," Clem cried. "Carried them without arms or legs through the fields of Dá Nang. And he's blubbering over a sup of blood?"

Dane was put in charge and people waited an hour, sometimes two, for their dinner. The clam steamers had to be axed from the menu and the garlic roasted red snapper. Bar food and to-go orders suspended. The children's menu chopped on weekends. One night, the gravel section walked out *en masse* with Clem leaping into the parking lot after them, cradling a tray of surf 'n turf, pony-tail and sarong soaring.

"What am I gonna do?" Flo dumped another plastic plate of untouched food. "How am I ever gonna save any money at this rate?"

"Hang in there." Priscilla's voice wafted out from the patio where she was arranging the weekly roster, allocating shifts according to who was kissing Clem's illustrious ass. "Dane will sort it out."

Flo felt his long arms cradle her from behind, his mouth brush the back of her neck. "How about some dark chocolate?" he whispered, his hands clasping her waist, as she leaned into him.

The August people poured in over the stretch, their cars lining both sides of the highway. The bar crowd spilled out to meet them causing traffic to slow down or stop altogether. Clem abandoned his perch on the tree stump and joined them.

"It's like a bloody cocktail party." He shrugged. "That's never gonna end."

"And we're more like cocktail waitresses." Flo stopped at the bar to pick up a tray of Bailey's Banana Coladas.

"Keep thinking of the dollar bills, babe," said Becky, knocking back a shot of Jack 'n ginger, spots of the amber liquid blotting the front of her FISH THIS top. "It don't matter how you're making 'em, they're your ticket outa here."

"Turn your tables, tables," Priscilla roared from the tree stump. "I need tables, tables."

After Labor Day, the season slowly screeched to a halt and within weeks, Clem was staggering up and down the side of the road, willing the cars to stop. The staff passed the time cleaning and catching up on daytime television.

Flo sprayed Windex on the kitchen window and shone until she could see her sad reflection against the sand dunes. She had wasted her time here and her time was a precious thing to be wasting. Just two more weekends. She'd give it one last push. But, what was she going to do then? Where was she going to go? That was the thing. Sometimes, it was just easier to stay.

The Oprah Show was interrupted by OJ Simpson's shiny face and a voice announcing 'not guilty.' Half the studio audience sat still in shock, the others erupted from their chairs, clapping and cheering. Behind her, some of the bar boys buried their heads in their hands, while diners looked on wide-eyed from the deck, their mouths open. Flo slipped into the kitchen to check on a *mussels marina* and found Dane and Priscilla embracing, the sisters jumping up and down screeching.

"Justice has been served," said Dane.

"Is that a new dish?" She giggled.

"Our brother is innocent." Priscilla said.

"You have another brother?"

"A black man got off with a white woman's murder." Priscilla's tone was icy.

"She was his wife," said Flo and a strained silence filled the room and followed her out the door.

Only ten people showed up for dinner that night and Clem pranced around the deck, his face red with rage. "I have more staff than customers," he cried, reaching across the bar for another Heineken. "One of you will have to go."

"How about Flo?" said Priscilla.

"Yeah Flo, you're fired." It was the first time he'd said her name.

Removing her apron without a word, she fixed her eyes on Becky's long braids hardly budging behind the bar. Her feet dragged across the deck, crunched into the gravel and towed her to her car. She peeled the Ford Chevrolet away from a dusty kerb and accelerated out onto the highway. Her heart didn't stop pounding until the narrow neck of sand with the roadside shack disappeared from her rear-view.

The clouds were sitting on the sky, the beachfront properties boarded-up and a sense of being cast adrift had descended on the stretch. Flo wandered in over the dunes to watch the summer people file out of town, an annual ritual of hers. Oprah was right, the only one wasting her time was herself.

"We're off to Aruba." Dane pulled up in Clem's wine red Cadillac and rolled down the window. "Priscilla and I are leasing a new restaurant there. It's the start of a dynasty."

"And Clem?"

YOU COULD'VE BEEN SOMEONE

"He's spending the winter in Philly, with his family. How about you?"

"Oh, I might head up to New York. Or Chicago. Had enough of this place."

"Don't forget to say goodbye." He started to drive away and stopped again. "Why don't you come to the wrap-up party?"

So, on the Monday night of Columbus weekend, Flo found herself back at the Fishy Fish House, the lights on the bushes a bracelet of coloured beads, the air rank with clams, the bar jamming, jamming.

"One of my best girls," she heard Clem say, as she nudged her way up to the counter. "Been with me for years," he said. "She's the best."

"He didn't even notice I was gone," she said to Becky.

"Don't even think about it." Becky was shaking her head, as she poured blobs of Pina Colada mixture into plastic cups.

Dane steered her onto the dancefloor, his mouth in her hair, Bob Marley *Jammin' Jammin'*, Priscilla standing at the kitchen door, pink lips parted and her chocolate brown eyes blank.

"They say if you go black," Dane whispered, "you'll never go back."

"Is that so?" said Flo.

Shortlisted Writing Spirit Award 2011

UNANSWERED PRAYERS

"What floor?" A tanned forefinger points at the button pad.

"Sixty-seventh," I say.

"Me too." Broad smile. White teeth. "How about that?" He shakes his head. "Haven't seen you around before."

"No, I'm just temping." I shrug. "For the week."

"Oh, which department?" He crumples his brow.

"Corporate Accounts," I say with a shiver, my desk in the clouds beckoning.

What possesses a girl who hates heights to take a job in a skyscraper? Spell it out. Scrapes. The. Sky. Needs must, Mam would say. And I needed to get out of waitressing. Jump on the corporate ladder. At home, they're hopping onto a property ladder. This man's legs are as long as ladders.

"How about that?" He's all smiles again. "I'm next door. Communications." He offers me a hand, the size of a malt shovel Dad would say, although I still haven't figured out what's the difference between a malt and any other sort of shovel.

"Sean Casey," he says.

"Carolyn Broderick."

"Gee, with an accent like that . . ." He leans against the wall, folding his arms. "I'd a thought you'd be a Bridget or a Kathleen."

"We have other names too, you know."

An all-over tan he has. Well, the bits I can see. Neck and face and the part not covered by a white starched shirt. Looks like the young exec types I saw roaming the office yesterday. Probably 'summers' in the Hamptons. Or, more like the wife and kids 'summer' and he catches up with them at weekends. In Manhattan, summer is a verb.

It's the same in Kilkee. Mothers and children huddle in a corner of the strand Monday to Friday hiding from the wind behind towels and rocks and other makeshift screens, waiting for Dad to come rescue them at the weekends. A place where there's sand in the sandwiches. In the bottles of Cidona too and in the seats of their wet bathing suits, along with the periwinkles. Summer is not a verb in County Clare, but a Proper Noun. No wonder I had to get outa there.

Thank you, God.

The carriage shudders. Stops. Flings me against his pinstriped chest. The lights flash, flicker, blink, black. Sixty-two bleeps red on the floor indicator. "What was that?" I pull away from his heartbeat. Regular

"Nothin'," he says, swishing his hand. "Don't worry hon."

I'm worried about being late for work. After all, it's only Tuesday. Want to make a good impression. Make it in Corporate.

You'll make loads of tips, people told me. And I did. Pounding across the tiled floors of the El Greco diner for twelve hours on the trot, if I did a double, I'd feel my feet swell. My sneakers hot, sweaty boats carrying me back and forth to the kitchen, the counter, the wait station, the hostess stand. My head hopping trying to remember orders, drinks, an extra straw, mayo on the side, toast no butter; burgers medium, rare, well done, black and blue; eggs over easy, sunny side up, scrambled, poached, egg white omelette, Benedict. At home, they were just fried.

"I'm Irish too," he says, flicking open his cell phone. A gold *Claddagh* glistens against the screen. The ring is a sure sign, of his ancestry and marital status.

"My folks came over after the Famine," he says, slouching down on his hunkers, his back against the wall. I'm getting used to the darkness now and can make out the form of him.

"How long you been here?"

"Ten minutes," I say.

"Huh?"

"Sorry. About ten years."
"About? Don't you know?"

Precise. Like George in the diner. At three o'clock, after the lunch madness ended, we could take a break, if we were on a double. I think I'll take a break now, I'd tell him, to be polite. You think? George was always gruff. Don't you know? I had to practice the words 'taking lunch now George'. Recite them, scurrying up and down three flights of stairs, hot plates balanced along my arm, burning the bend of my elbow, my wrist and the palms of my hands. I practiced being assertive, precise.

"Nine years and eleven months," I say. "I landed on October the eleventh, 1991."

It was a beautiful blue day, like today, the sun shining, warm against my skin. That's what I loved about New York, its brightness all year round. At home, it was just grey. It was a quiet autumn afternoon in the Bronx when I stepped out of the subway station for the first time and sank into a carpet of leaves. The sidewalk covered in them, the sky a kaleidoscope of colour. Yellow, rust, vermillion, green, at home they were just green, fluttered from the trees to my feet. Must be why they call it the fall, I figured.

"Gee, you're somethin' else," he says. "I was born in Brooklyn and moved no further than Farmingdale." His phone chirrups. He flicks it open. Someone is screaming. "What's up, hon?" he says. "A plane crash?" I hear the phone die. "Sucks," he says.
"Something wrong?"
"Nah, just my assistant." He snaps the phone shut. "Somethin' about a plane crash. These bimbos get excited about nothin'. Welcome to Corporate America."

You'd do great in Corporate, one of my regulars used to say. As if Corporate was a diner down the street where they served Panini and wraps instead of tuna melt on rye. All you have to do is show up on time and they'd be excited, he said. But, I've no computer experience, I said, even though I was dying for a way out of there. Prayed for it every night. Please God. Like I did back in sunny Kilkee. The way you tot up those checks in your head, Mr. Regular said regularly, you could learn. He had a point. El Greco almost closed down when the calculators didn't work. And you can multi-task too, he said. It's true. I could deliver food to table ten, drop a check on nine, clear away seven and re-set eight, while hollering 'anything to drink?' at table two by the window, all the time praying the order would be ready for the deuce on one by the time I got back to the hatch. Never make an idle journey, George told me, and I didn't.

"Pray they'll fix the lift soon," I say to the tanned man. I can make out his face now, the white teeth. "I don't want to be late my second day." There was a rumbling out in the hallway.

"Pray? Lift?" He frowns. "How do you speak so fast without gettin' your lips in a mess? And, aren't there too many verbs there?"

Try 'summer.'

"The elevator, lift. Whatever. Say a prayer it'll be fixed soon."

"Oh, I don't pray, hon. This is America. Everything gets fixed." He clicks a brown finger and thumb. "Like magic. No need to pray." He slumps to the floor, pats a place beside him. "Sit down," he says. "Relax."

I'm prancing back and forth in the dark and have no intention of relaxing. It sounds like they're moving furniture over our heads and hurling it down the stairs.

"Do you have family here?" he asks.

"No. Just me."

"Married? Divorced?"

"Neither." This gets them every time. Americans try it at least once. Marriage is a rite of passage for them. Drugs too. Everyone here has snorted cocaine by the time they graduate High School.

"How come?"

"Dunno." I fold into my hunkers. "Never got around to it."
That throws them too. As if marriage was a movie I hadn't
managed to catch.

"For real?" He checks the Casio G-Shock watch on his brown
wrist. Glows 08.59. Digital. "Geez," he says. "We are gonna be
late. Boss won't like that."

"Won't they understand when we tell them what happened?"

"Nah. They don't give a rat's ass about excuses, hon. Just
dollars." His fingernail scrapes across my neck. "It's cut throat
out there." It brushes against the ends of my hair. "Get out, as
soon as you can." It traces my lips. "Wish I only had one week."
It grazes my cheek. "Like you."

I wish I could stand up, but my knees are stuck.

"And I wish I could stay in the same place forever," I say.

What's wrong with the coleslaw, table three asks? Nothing, I
said. Did they change it? I don't think so, sir. Why fix something
that's not broken? I don't think it is fixed, sir, and it wasn't
broken, but I'll get you another one, just in case. I walked away
with his side dish. I'm having a conversation about coleslaw.
Secretary to a CEO back in Shannon, I spent my days typing
Minutes, arranging meetings, setting up interviews, taking
phone calls, making phone calls, writing up Reports and then
the company pulled out of town. Next thing I know, I'm talking
about coleslaw. Whisking off my apron, I told George I was
leaving. Don't take that dish with you, he roars, as I dump its
contents in table three's crotch. Fix this, I said and left. Don't
come back, I could hear George screaming all along Lexington
Avenue. And I didn't.

"We're never happy," I say to Sean Casey, my backside
touching the elevator floor.

"I guess not," he says and sighs. "Take my wife now. Work
my ass off to give her everything. And she wants more. Now
she's talking about a home in the Hamptons. Who's she kiddin'?
I've never been as far as the Jersey Shore and she wants a home in
the Hamptons. On what I earn? The kids too are always lookin'

for somethin'. I feel like disappearing. Never coming back. See how the bitch would manage then without my mediocre pay check." His tone is acid. Un-American.

If I ever get out of here, I might disappear myself. Go back home. Take a computer course. Buy a house. Things are improving over there. Plenty of work, they say. Plenty of nice office jobs for nice girls like me. And people keep to themselves. Don't tell you their life stories in diners, in elevators. Don't even call them elevators.

"What's a pretty girl like you do without a husband?" His breath is peppermint. I imagine his lips warm and hard, only inches from mine.

My breathing stalls a nanosecond. *Please God.*

Tanned fingers circle my ankle. "Maybe I can hook you up with something more permanent."

I exhale stac-ca-to.

Please. God.

The tanned hand cups the curve of my calf. "You'd be good in Communications," he says. "You're tough. Gutsy. I like that in a woman."

Please. God.

Brown knuckles gently pummel my inner thigh. "I might be needing a new assistant."

Please. God.

My knee jerks.

Jerk.

Perspiration beads my brow. His knuckles are skimming my nipples now and my heart stops, I'm sure.

Please. God. A mir-a-cle.

The doors swing open without warning. I spring into standing position and leap into the lobby. Into a stampede of footsteps. Smoke. A cacophony of sound. Crying. Choking. Loudspeakers screeching. Bodies wedged into the stairwell. Fire-fighters trundling upwards. NYPD. Paramedics.

Magic.

"Catch you later, hon." I hear a voice boom above me. "Gonna walk up the last few flights," he says, struggling against the crowd. White teeth, pinstripe chest, brown shovel hands disappear into a cloud of grey smoke.

Cut-throat.

Thank you, God.

A navy blue uniform with sunrise red hair takes my hand and links me to a line of people filing down the stairway. "Don't look back," she says. And I don't.

Shortlisted Cork CoCo 'From the Well' Anthology 2012

AROUND THE BEND

It was January when Deborah moved onto Broadway and Van Cortlandt was covered in snow. The park's milky landscape clouded her window, its squiggles of bare trees like something a child would draw. The weather was frigid that first week with wind chills plunging below zero. She watched Wheel of Fortune every night and ate take-away from the downstairs deli, an unopened storage box her table. Hissing radiators muffled sounds from adjacent apartments, but not the screeching of quiz show contestants. Flicking through a book on creative visualisation, she learnt that she could make of life what she wanted. Imagine that? 'Don't let your imagination run away with you,' her Mom used to say, back when Deborah wished something would.

Green blades of grass started to sprout across the park. Coffee, dark no sugar, appeared on the deli counter, as she swept through its glass doors every morning. Lola's Laundromat was in full spin and K9 Grooming about to open its doggy flap. Deborah stomped down the subway stairs and jostled for a plastic carroty seat. The Number 1 train took her into Harlem in twenty-two minutes giving her time to breathe before Sophomore Business; time to daydream about class plans for alphabetical filing. Daydream about something better, the book said.

Slinking home past The Bend every evening, she saw the boys gather about the bar, heard their laughter echo onto the sidewalk and felt their eyes follow her from window to window. Love is coming to me easily and effortlessly, she circled Van Cortland later, easily and effortlessly.

Billy used see her trot by all togged out in a suit and briefcase. Heard her in the deli too, her voice velvety and smooth, not grating on his earlobes like most Yanks. Caught her cross the road later in her sweats, the tits standing up like soldiers through the fleece. She'd a fine rack for one so small and he swore her eyes lingered a little longer on his when they flickered by the window. He didn't usually go for redheads. Then again, didn't know if she really was a red one. Only one way to find out.

"Can I ask you a personal question?" He blocked her path on the sidewalk, grey clouds low in the sky, more of an Irish day than the ones he was used to in the Bronx.

"Sure," she said, her eyes green, her freckles spare, her full lips painted pink.

He'd intended asking what bra size she wore; if she'd had a good ride lately. "You're the spit of Bette Midler," he said, sucking on a cigarette.

"Is that a question?" She gave him the quizzical eye.

He flicked ash on the ground and turned on the hard heels of his boot. "I think she's lovely," he said, vanishing into the bar.

Deborah played with the word all the way up four flights of stairs. Mom said it all the time too. A melted cheese, a new frock, a day off school, even a warm whiskey was lovely.

On St. Patrick's Day he was on the sidewalk again. She'd been cooped up in the apartment all day correcting index cards and was in dire need of coffee. "Why aren't you at the parade?" he asked. She couldn't tell him she had no one to go with. After all, this was her country. She couldn't admit she was all alone on a street where he knew everyone.

He stubbed out a cigarette with the toe of his Timberland. Thirties, bald as an egg, Andre Agassi with heavy eyes and a two-day beard. A hard nut, Mom would say.

"You're welcome to join me and the lads, if you like," he said, a cell phone chirping in his hand. He flipped it open and walked away. It was hard to believe that an invitation had been proffered, much less considered.

She slouched towards the deli, took a sip of the murky brown liquid and felt it burn a path deep into her belly, disappointment vying for attention in her veins with the caffeine. Life is not about 'should haves' the book said, and he hadn't asked her outright. Irishmen are never direct was all Mom had to say when Dad left without a word. This one said she was lovely though. Indirectly.

By Easter, there was a stretch to the day, leaves on the trees and a warm breeze blowing along Broadway. Sophomores had mastered filing and were tackling the keyboard. 'FRF space, JUJ space,' Deborah chanted, as glossy fingernails hopped off the keys, staccato. Twenty pairs of eyes stared at spanking new computer screens, as she held their attention for the first time in twelve weeks.

"Doin' anything for the holiday, Miss?" One of them asked. Big hair. Eyeliner.

"Oh, hanging out with family, and friends," she said.

"That's good. You deserve it, Miss."

"We don't get what we deserve," Deborah told her. "We get what we believe."

The girl's eyebrows shot up. "Why did you become a teacher, Miss?"

"No reason."

"You could've done much better, you know."

Trees clustered Van Cortlandt like clumps of broccoli, steam belched out of Lola's and the dogs were hot out of K9 Grooming. She sauntered up from the subway and saw the doors of the Bend flung open onto Broadway.

"Join us for a cocktail," the barmaid said, waving her inside.

Before the words slid out of her mouth, Deborah was sliding onto a barstool, ordering a white wine spritzer and watching the way the soda sparkled in the tall glass when she heard, "Are you cold, or just glad to see me?"

If he stood at a certain angle, behind her right shoulder, with his arm along the back of her stool, Billy could gaze at her tits. All night long. Without her even knowing. Debs had an innocence about her. Something a lot of the Irish girls lost, as soon as they spun through the revolving doors of JFK.

"Robert William," he said, showing her his left palm. "A bloody English name, I tell the auld one. But, here they call me . . ."

"Billy," she said. "Nice meeting you."

"Go King," the boys chanted. "You're the king."

"King's the name and King's the man." He puffed out his *Nás na Rí* sweatshirt. "I was even reared in the town of Kings. Speak the Gaelic too and I graduated High School. Right Ellie?"

"Huh!" The barmaid slammed two more drinks on the counter. "A high school in the mountains more like."

"Well, I can quote Patrick Kavanagh." He placed a fist on his heart and recited a few lines of poetry. Deborah caught the words *barn dance* and *bicycles*.

"That's lovely," said a lady sipping sherry. "I used cycle to the dances at home, long ago."

"Ah! Mammy, and I used walk out with women like you." He draped an arm around her. "And all that kissin' would have me in a muck of sweat by the time we got to her door."

"When did you cop on?" one of the lads asked.

"Lost me oats when I was nineteen, I did." Billy paraded up and down the bar. "Up against the range in me mother's kitchen." He stopped beside Deborah. "Never had a problem pulling birds after that."

"Liar," said Ellie in that casual tone they shared. Their vowels broad and flat like the singers on Dad's long-playing records. Irish music was so sad already, made Mom want to slice her wrists wide open.

"Liars have legs," sherry lady said, inserting coins into the jukebox.

Are you lonesome tonight? Billy took Deborah's hand and led her onto the dance floor. His hands on her waist, he rested his head against hers. "So soft," she whispered, her fingers stroking the down that covered his scalp.

"The only thing soft about me," he said. "But, women won't believe that." He smelt of cigarette smoke and Paco Rabane after-shave.

Debs taught school, he laid bricks; she read books, he rode a motorbike; she sipped wine, he supped beer, too much of it really. He pulled away and gave the counter a kick, whinnied like a horse. "You need a man to mind you," he said. "But, I'm not up to the job."

What is right for me will come to me; Deborah tapped out the forty-two steps to her door. Slid between her apricot sheets and stared at the dill pickle walls, the high white ceiling in her Feng Shui, green for sleep, bedroom. If only she'd held on a bit longer, let him know she liked him. Leave no stone unturned, Mom would say. If only Mom had left a note, said goodbye, given some indication. If only Dad hadn't gone back to the girl he always went back to. If only is lonely reeled around in her head.

She could hear the hum of a TV, the distant swish of a shower, water gurgling through the pipes. Later, she heard voices on the stairs, the floorboards creak, someone slump against her door, turn on the landing. She heard whispering, a door banging and feet shuffling across the ceiling.

Deborah tied a knot in her sarong, tugged at her floppy hat and crossed the street from the park. It was warm for April with temperatures heading for a record thirty. Ellie had a stemmed glass of wine bubbling on the bar by the time she walked across the tiled floor. "This is with Billy." She winked.

I love and approve of myself, love and approve.

"Love the skirt," he said, cigarette at the side of his mouth.

Is it sexy? Sexy? Say it's sexy, Billy.

"It's you," he said.

Deep she was; those green eyes always somewhere else. It would take a man miles to reach her. Part of him wanted it and part of him was terrified.

"Gimme some mother's milk." He nodded at Ellie.

"Watch how a man treats his mother," said the sherry lady, "because that's how he'll treat you too."

"Crazy," Ellie muttered, pulling the pint, more like a milkmaid with the doughy arms, buttery hair. "When you see crazy coming cross the street."

"What's a fine woman doin' alone on Easter Sunday?" Billy asked Deborah.

"I'm not alone now," she said.

There were Christmas lights dangling from the ceiling fan; shamrocks tossed across the jukebox; a witch's hat perched nonchalantly on top of the till. There was the sun sinking behind the trees casting a tangerine glow on the park, the lads cranking up the banter, Ellie keeping the beers coming, the coins coming for the jukebox, the billiards table, the cigarette machine. And there was Billy drawing Deborah to him like a flame.

I feel it, I feel it and if I feel it, it's real.

"I feel a stirrin'," he said. "It won't be long before you and I shift."

If you do what you always do, you'll get what you always got. How about now?" she asked him. "Or is that too pushy?"

"Pushy is good," he said.

Two sets of footsteps tapped it up the stairs, two bodies slid between the apricot sheets, two heads burrowed into the peach pillows. "Duvets make me horny," Billy said, pulling it over them, kissing her hair, her neck, her eyelids, her lips, shyly cupping her breasts, slipping into her with a tenderness she'd never before known. He cradled her in his arms afterwards, circling her inner thigh with his thumb. Mom once said that a man's true nature comes out in bed.

"You're so light," he said. "Like a butterfly."

She smiled, slotting into him. *Some people have this their whole lives.*

"The other one has me back nearly broken."

She held her breath. "Other? One?"

"The one that helps me clean out the pipes."

Deborah thought for a minute he was talking about the radiators, or the second-rate sewerage system that snaked through her apartment walls.

"Been throwing the leg over her for years," he said, his thumb rotating around and around her thigh. "Lights up like a Christmas tree when I say I'll marry her, but she might dump me once she gets the Green Card and we can't have that. So," he took his thumb away and clasped his hands behind his head. "I've all the benefits without the paperwork."

When people tell you who they are, believe them.

"You're kiddin' me," she said.

He rolled off the bed, taking sheets with him, dragged on his jeans and legged it to the door. In Debs's world, people have room in their houses, fathers come home with the wages and mothers are free with the hugs. She wasn't crammed three to a bed listening to fights through thin walls. Didn't have to protect herself from an auld one, didn't have to belt her with a Hurley stick and wasn't put away in Reform. "I might call," he said, fumbling with the doorknob, "then again, I might not." The floorboards groaned on the landing. "I'd only take you down with me," he said, his words whistling through the stairwell, her heart descending each step with him.

I am worth loving, worth loving, worth loving.

She strolled up from the subway; the sun pressing down on her head, ruffled the dogs outside K9, half-waved at the girls in Lola's and met Ellie sweeping the sidewalk.

"You should never have let him know you liked him," Ellie said.

"I thought he liked me too."

"Billy takes to everyone, but no one in particular."

"He said he has someone else," Deborah looked towards the window, tried to make out its shapes and shadows, saw her hair wide and woolly; eyes puffed and red-rimmed. "An old boot," she said. "A tart that even the tide wouldn't take out. But, the book says . . ."

"Don't mind that book." Ellie swished her broom in a semi-circle over the block. "You can do better than this."

This or something better . . .

She heard voices on the landing later, someone thud against her door, heard the floorboards creaking, as the night closed in on Broadway.

"Her mother was mad," she heard Ellie say.

"Kicky mare, kicky foal," Billy said and Ellie laughed.

She's leaving today and he never said goodbye. Heading Upstate he's heard, some place classy, Billy bets. He hasn't seen her since the night he had his way with her; gave her pleasure; made her squirm. He never called. Never does. Even when he says he will, even when he wants to. Even when he meets one he'd like to meet again, he never calls. Women. They'd break a whore's heart. Emotions are all in the head anyhow. Nearest he ever got was Debs.

He hears the door shove open. Sees the boys swivel their thick heads, hears her voice loud and cheery, unfamiliar.

"I'm off now," she says.

"Is that the smell?" He tries to laugh, but can't, leaves it to the lads instead.

"Imagine that," says Ellie, topping up a white wine with soda water.

"I did," says Debs, looking at him, ignoring the drink.

She backs away then, all the time looking at him. "In our endings are our beginnings," she says, slamming the door.

The park is floodlit with garish street lamps and a sliver of moon hooks onto the sky. Picnickers are packing up for the day and a lone jogger circles the track. A cab pulls up outside and she swings those fine shanks into the front seat. Billy tips it to the window, tries to shout 'Deb-or-ah,' but it comes out in a cry, a whimper. The car screeches around the bend. Broadway is still for a second, the bar behind him quiet. He rests his head against the glass.

"There's a pint here with your name on it." Ellie claps her hands. "Someone play a song on the jukebox. We'll do a line of white powder, dance."

He turns around slowly and whinnies, kicks the counter with his Timberland boot, drops an arm over sherry lady's shoulder.

"I did a line once," she says, patting his head.

He raises his glass at the boys.

"Go king," they chant.

Shortlisted Trevor/Bowen 2013

KITTY'S HOMECOMING

K itty couldn't wait to get home. She couldn't wait to stroll through the streets of her childhood, to feel part of a place instead of always being out of it. And she couldn't wait to hold her baby again. It was all she could think about really, rummaging around her little home in Hackney. It had been a fine flat when she and Bud moved in, when their number had come up on the Council list. Then the area started to go down, you see, as did most of East London. She wouldn't put a dog in it now.

Gangs congregating at the foot of the stairwell squabbling and drinking and doing their drugs, sniggering when she slouched by laden down with groceries. Or worse still, with Bud slumped against her. She wouldn't venture out after two o'clock in the afternoon. A stranger she still was, in a land she hadn't chosen. A land she'd had to get used to. Like she got used to Bud. She'd been propping him up for forty years now. Half a lifetime really.

"You wanted someone to mind," the counsellor said, "after you lost the baby."

It wasn't that she lost him; it was more that she couldn't find him. She'd held him next to her heartbeat for seven months, felt him suck at her nipple, his tiny hands curl around her fingers. He'd gurgled and kicked at the bedclothes every morning when she bent over his cot. Nobody was ever so glad to see her before. Not her mother, whose heart she broke when she said she was expecting. Not her father who didn't have a heart, who couldn't look her in the eye when she walked out the door. They would never be able to hold their heads up again, they said, if she brought the boy home. Hers was cast downwards when they pulled him from her. People had no feelings back then, you see, and hers had been numbed.

She left on the boat then with the rest of the herd. Droves of girls had their brood beyond, others were rid of them before they had a chance at life. She saw them pour into Euston Station with the Legion of Mary flocking around them like crows, eager to save their souls. She'd left hers behind.

She called him after her Dad in the end, but left him with a whole heap of other names, 'bastard' and 'illegitimate' among them. She looked for him then in her dreams; fancied she saw him on the tube screeching through the underground, under an unused bench in Hyde Park, running along a corridor in a Hammersmith hospital, sitting at a table in a Kentish Town café.

Every night she was looking, looking, looking for a baby and every morning she awoke in an empty bed.

Bud told her she was raving, that she was losing the run of herself. She'd lost everything else, might as well lose that too. He had to carry his crippled father up to bed on his back every night. Was forced to leave home at fourteen and find solace on the building sites of Birmingham. He was called Paddy and Mick, and lots of other names besides, while she'd answered to a roll call in a cosy convent school. Had to eat cold spam sandwiches in his digs of an evening and buy drink for the subbies in British bars, while she was fed and founded on a Dublin Corporation estate. Had to contend with cruel landladies while she'd slept in a nice room above a London pub; served ale and smiles to lonely Irishmen; probably gave them more than that too. Kitty knew the ranting was because he was hollow too. Everyone who took that boat brought with them a bag full of dreams. She could see it in their Irish eyes. Everywhere else they could change who they were, but not on the streets of London.

Her night-time ramblings ended when she took the counselling. She'd seen the telephone number at the end of the Magdalene laundry film. Coiled her fingers around the thick black chord of the telephone and dragged it towards her. Hordes of Irish girls all over the world dialled those digits, even though they didn't all give birth amid unwashed linen. Kitty's labour ward was in a Home among the fertile fields of Meath where the nuns were as cruel and as unfeeling as their washroom sisters. They plucked the child from her arms without a smile or a comforting word and banged the door behind her. For years, she'd dragged her feet through London, her heart leaden from that one mistake.

"There's no such thing as a mistake," the counsellor said. "Everything is for a reason."

Reason? Reason? What reason, Kitty wondered, what reason for this? Did God have a reason or the priest for that matter? She hadn't spoken to either in years. Hadn't sat in a church unless it was empty. She knew their words could not fill the place where her dreams used to dwell. She settled for memories instead.

She sat beside the window at night looking at the sky, thinking about how that same sky sheltered Ireland. The same moon shone there, the same stars scattered that same dark blanket over Dublin. When her Dad died and left her the house he'd once run her from, she got the notion then for coming home. There was nothing to keep her in England once she'd stopped working, you see. That was why they all went in the first place, wasn't it, and some of them had such a time of it really, dancing every night. There was any amount of men in London after the War. Wall-to-wall Irishmen too. It would be no bother finding a husband. There was no missing home then.

It all ended soon enough – the dancing, the work, and the hope of romance. Not even the husband had turned up. Only Bud. He'd never married her because he had a wife, you see, and what would he want with another one? They lived under the brush some said, living in sin it was called long ago. Her partner he was now, but there wasn't a name for him back then. There wasn't a name for men who lived with women who weren't their wives. He became her buddy then, Bud for short.

There were plenty of names for Kitty. Damaged goods, a cut loaf, a hussy, a harlot, an unmarried mother. She could take her pick. She never took to any of them. A lone parent she would be called now, a solitary yet nicer sound. No man would look at her she was told, they wouldn't give her the time of day or a second glance. No man wanted a slice out of a cut loaf and the ones that did said she wouldn't miss it anyhow. That's why she fell for Bud, you see, when he stumbled into The Railway Bar on Liverpool Street. He threw a fiver on the counter and said he wished he had her looks and her money. That's all it took. She always said she would never let another man touch her, unless with gold, but no ring had passed her finger, yet. Bud had made her feel part of a whole again, and that had been enough, for a while.

She packed their belongings into a cardboard box and they took the plane home. Bud's hairy arm trapped her, his whiskey breath was suffocating. She asked the Air Hostess to open a window and Bud barked at her not to be stupid. He'd knocked back a bottle to calm his nerves; Kitty had nothing to quiet hers.

When they landed she wanted to pinch the ground with her toes; take a deep breath and inhale the fresh Irish air; embrace another human being; experience some physical sense of coming home. Instead, she was hurried on by the surge of the crowd behind her and Bud pulling her by the coat sleeve, afraid to let go.

They were hurled into a city they didn't recognize and devoured by its citizens who were no longer familiar. She felt like a ghost curving its shadowy streets, invisible, fluid, unknown. It would take a while to get used to, but then England had too. The soot and the grime of its cities had jolted them out of the complacent green fields of Ireland half a century before. There too, she had strayed through streets where she was not known. At least here, she hoped to blend in one day. She hoped to belong.

Bud had her all wired up at first, because he wasn't able for the move, he said, not after fifty years away. Once again, she'd settled for a strange land. She hadn't been back in over a decade, not since the funeral when she watched them shovel clay onto her Dad's coffin, when she had tried to grieve for his passing. She hadn't noticed the shifting landscape then, only the erratic pace of her pulse counting out the loss of what might have been. Coming home for good was different. It was like emigrating all over again. The exile is always suspended between two worlds, always the outsider. But, she's near the baby now, you see, and that's all that matters.

She searches for him in every schoolyard, in every young boy's face, in the misty features of adolescents, in the bearded jaws of young men, even in the silver hair of their fathers. She seeks in them all that she has missed. All the years that have rolled by when she was away, all of the history that she was not part of. Her boy tramps these thoroughfares, she's sure, and maybe they've met already. Brushed shoulders in the queue for Superquinn or sat side-by- side on the LUAS. Sauntered along Sandymount strand together or shared the DART into Connolly station. At best, they've watched the Nine O'clock news at the same time, or *Prime Time*, and she longs to ask him who everyone is because she doesn't know anymore.

Bud hates the changes. "They're all bad," he says, "like the people." Arrogant, loud-mouthed individuals storm the streets of his boyhood, never stopping to ask how he is. Don't know who he is, don't care either. "They're all taken up with money," he says. "Greed and new cars with the year blazed on them for all to see. Show-offs who don't even know what's good for them; who've never done a hard day's work since they were born. Nothing but cranes dot the Irish horizon now," he says. "Cranes and currency."

"We lifted buildings in Britain," Kitty tells him, "but not our heads. Cranes do both for us here."

"They'll all come crashing down some day," he forecasts. "Wait 'til you see."

Kitty loves the noise and the colours and the confidence of the people. She loves being misunderstood and mistaken. She asks questions in an accent that says she should know, but doesn't, and feels lost in a city that should be familiar, yet isn't. Still, she's glad she gave her son this land on his birthday with all its shades of imperfection; glad he didn't have to grow up in a place where he was out of place. She knows where he is now, you see. She knows his name, where he lives, where he works; that he's married and has children with faces just like his. He might look for his history in them, but can only find it in hers.

Bud is doped from the whiskey tonight the way Kitty used to be by her dreams. She's been minding him for forty years now, but tomorrow that might change. Tomorrow she will see her son. The Social Worker's voice is curt and crisp. They will convene at her office, have tea and Kitty is to be prepared for a show of emotion. He will read letters she'd written explaining why she'd kept him so long; how she couldn't let him go; that she'd given him up and then wanted him back again; how she'd kept changing her mind. In the end, she couldn't take him away from his new mother, she will explain, the way they'd tugged him from her. She worries that he's better educated; from a different class; that he might be ashamed of her. No matter.

Tomorrow it will all be sorted. She will lace her fingers through his, straighten his tie, dust down his suit, gaze into his eyes and see her reflection there. She will know who she is, at last. She will know who he is too and they will no longer have to pass each other by on strange streets. Tomorrow Kitty is coming home, you see, and she can't wait.

HerStory 2010 & Ireland's Own August 2012

ORANGE YOU GLAD?

It jumps off the page at her, the orange Radley bag – an inner beauty, the ad says. Sure who'll ever see her insides? Fina pushes open the door of Shangri-La and takes a deep breath. Her Higher Power is very proud, but her Inner Child is throwing its usual tantrum. Not fair, not fair, not fair. If only she could stay young and beautiful forever, without someone sticking needles in her face.

"Can I help you," a voice says. Pink lips full, creamy skin, flaxen yellow hair, a starched uniform, chalk white, straining around the curves of her young body. The only colour is in the sign above her head – *drinking cherry juice keeps you young.*

"I have an appointment," Fina says. "With . . . em . . . em . . ." She fishes for a business card in her handbag.

"Emily?" the girl says.

"No, Niamh." Fina hands her the card, trying to act nonchalant, as if this is an everyday occurrence for her, as if it's a devil-may-care kind of thing to do.

"I love that bit of devilment in you," Oisin used to say when she met him first, and she'd kept it going long after he stopped remarking.

"Oh, that's me," the snow queen shrieks, a little too cheery, or is it cherry, for Fina, this hour of the morning.

Niamh ushers her into a room, white again, except for the shiny stainless steel instruments on a stainless steel tray. Reminds her of a fertility clinic she'd run out of once. "Sit here," says the slip of a girl, patting a table-bed covered in tissue paper.

"Let me have a look." She pokes at Fina's face, now that Fina's settled with her two legs dangling a couple of inches above the white, tiled floor.

"Well, first of all, these need to go." She stretches the sides of Fina's eyes with her fingers, her breath so close, Fina can smell Listerine and clove drops.

"Yeah," she says. "Some crow left his footprints there without me noticing."

"Laughter lines, OK." Niamh makes serious notes on her jotter. "And I think this." She measures with a miniature ruler the space above Fina's nose. "No sense in walking around looking furious when you're happy, now is there?" The girl stares at Fina.

Oisin took her whole head in his hands once and examined every bit of it, his eyes watery. "I think I'm falling in love," he'd said.

"There isn't a fear of it." She'd thumped him in the chest. "Lust is more like it."

His face flooded with disappointment and she's never been able to get him to say it, since.

"And these." Niamh points at the corners of her mouth.

Fina tries to set her lips in a line, tries not to curl them into a smile. This is serious business, after all.

"That's it," Niamh exclaims, slapping down the notebook on the table. "How about you?" She pockets the pen and ruler. "What do you think?" This from a woman who looks like she's never laughed, cried, or had a single meaningful thought her whole life.

"Oh, whatever you think yourself," she says, wishing there was an operation for assertiveness.

"You have beautiful eyes, you know." Niamh is still examining her. "A lovely smile too. And what a great head of hair."

Fina loops one of her curls behind her ear. They're still light and fluffy, caramel. Oisin likes to rake his fingers through them until they lie like corkscrews on the pillow. Is it natural, people ask her all the time. How can hair not be?

"Thanks," she says to the fair Niamh.

She'd been shocked watching Law 'n Order the week before, on Halloween of all nights. The Special Victims Unit it was, and a sixty-year old woman, they kept calling her, was portrayed as old and lonely and odd. A shabby old lady whom the other characters addressed as 'Miss' and treated with trepidation. Fina started talking to the television; called Captain Cragen a moron; told him it was about time he retired. How could his detectives buy into this shit? Especially Olivia Benson. After all, isn't sixty the new forty? She was yelling, 'c'mon Liv,' confident she couldn't be heard in the apartment next door. The writers should be strung up, she roared, along with the producer, Dick Wolf.

She shut up when she spotted the picture of her and Oisin lolling against her bedside lamp. She saw the fine lines, the puckered brow, the lips fading from lack of colour, his boyish face next to hers.

After a sleepless night, she had dialled the number for Shangri-La.

When Niamh leaves to check the appointment book, Fina studies a chart on the wall - a colour wheel with definitions underneath. Orange is the colour of change, it states, like the amber in traffic lights. There is huge aggression in the orange and red wing. They symbolize spirituality, exude warmth and are flamboyant. Orange is the colour of the sun. It boosts appetite. Think breakfast foods, like orange juice and marmalade, to kick-start the day.

Knock, knock, is one of Oisin's childish jokes. Who's there? Banana. Banana who? Knock, knock. Who's there? Banana. Banana who? She's always right on cue. Knock, knock. Who's there? Banana. Banana who? She'd be getting fed up at this point. Knock, knock. Who's there? Orange. Orange who? Orange you glad I didn't say banana?

I am ablaze, she writes in her gratitude journal, her feet still dangling over the side of the table-bed. I rage and burn and ravage. I am searing, scorching, aflame. The sun caressing your bones; fruit juice dribbling down your chin; an ice-pop cooling your tongue, quenching your parched throat. I am your sunset, sunrise, your sky at night, your fire first thing in the morning.

"Unless these," she says when Niamh returns, tracing the lines on her forehead with her pen. "Or this." She taps her nose with a coral nail. "Or I don't suppose you can get rid of these?" She pinches the creases of fat at the curve of her jaw. She's on fire now, smoking, and she's gonna get her money's worth.

"No worries," says Niamh. "It'll be easy."

Fina is warming to her.

"You'll be looking hot in no time." The girl smiles at her and Fina smiles back, blushing, and she could swear there's a spot of pink in the girl's cheeks too.

"I'm cold," she'd said to Oisin that first morning she woke up in his flat.

"I think you're hot," he'd said, enveloping her in his arms. "A hot bit of stuff," he whispered, before ravaging her all over again, worshipping her with his body, he'd called it. She hadn't believed him at the time. And now?

"By the way," Niamh says, after they'd arranged an appointment and Fina is turning towards the door. "Love the bag."

"It's not too . . . ?"

"Nah." Niamh flaps a white hand. "You're as young as the man you're feeling."

Orange, Fina was about to say, stepping out into the sunlight. She flicks open her phone and scrolls down to O.

March 2013

STICKS AND STONES

It's windy today, blowing sand in my face, cutting it like a stone. I sit here on top of a hill and wonder which way to turn. Look into the rays of the sun. They do not sting. They do not burn.

"Never let them know you care," Mama used to say, before she stopped saying anything at all. She meant boys at the time. Boys I might like, boys who might like me, boys who might want to hold me in the night. All the wanting is gone now. Men have seen to that.

I see my village smouldering in the distance, a collection of huts, now the dying embers of your fire. The valley is dotted with houses. Small, flat-roofed, white. I would like some day to visit your land, knock at your door, sit at your table, sip your water and taste your fruit. I would like to come live with you. But, I can't let you know you have something I might want.

I heard gunfire when the night was still, heard your bombs explode and ignite, light up the sky. I smelt your smoke when the moon was a belly, heavy and full. Mine as flat as a board. Stick thin, they say I am. I saw my sisters' eyes full of fear; my mother's brave, yours angry and cruel, full of knowing what you were about to do. I heard you hiss and hold your breath; heard you sigh when you slapped me; froth at the mouth, as you removed your belt; heard you inhale when you had your way with me. I lay there like a stick, my heart a stone.

I felt you rip my dress, as you rolled away, your eyes still on me. But, you could not see me, for I have no soul. I didn't cry, or hold my breath, or sigh. There was no foam for my parched lips to lick when all your fumbling was done.

You called me bitch, *puta*, whore. As if it was my fault you couldn't come. Couldn't come to that place deep inside, which has ceased to be. Words won't hurt me, Mama said. They're all I've left of her now.

I was born in these hills, a daughter of the desert, the sand is in my bones.

"Be proud of your homeland," Mama would say. "Hold your head up high."

Still, there is no public outcry when I die, when my limbs are snapped like the branches of the pine tree, when my eyes are plucked from their holes, when a hand reaches in and rips out my heart. No sirens scream. No one prays at my burial place. There are no flowers where I lie.

Yet, I am you and you are me. I am your sister, mother and child. We are all threads of the Universe. What you feel, I feel, but do not show. My blood runs just as red as yours.

A woman of the wind I am, nameless, faceless, heartless, whore.

You made Mama beg and plea and grovel, made her crawl clinging to your boots. "Spare my children," she cried. Spoil the rod. Don't let them know, I tried to tell her, tried to catch her eye the colour of the sea when it's wild, don't let them know you care. But, it was too late. Pride deserts us when we're already down.

She made her people proud instead, made another martyr for them to praise.

It's my mind I have made up now, stumbling across the sand, listening for her voice in the wind. I run towards her, arms outstretched, not knowing what she says, struck deaf I am, deaf as stone. I am coming Mama, coming, I cry, another stick for your fire. Do not throw your words at me, I beg, for they cannot sting, they do not burn.

Your proud desert daughter I am, Mama, and I won't fall . . . won't fall . . . won't fall.

May 2013

Used

Maeve rinsed the wine glasses, emptied the ashtrays, filled up the dishwasher with the week's dishes and discarded the take-away containers. She'd had her blow-dry, bath and manicure and she'd changed the sheets. Just in case. A car rolled into the driveway, the radio murmuring. The dog hobbled out of his basket, tail wagging. Jack boomeranged back into their lives, like he did every Friday.

'Hon-ney, I'm ho-ome.' She heard him hollering.

In her head.

Jack didn't do holler.

"Hi," he said, his voice quiet, reliable. Calm in a crisis, her mother had said. "How's things?" He threw keys, coat, and a small canvas suitcase onto a nearby chair.

"Grand," she told him. "Dinner's ready." She patted his arm hoping for a frisson of electricity.

"Fish?" He eyed the salmon, pink on the plate. "That's three times this week, for me."

"Sorry," she said. "I didn't know."

By the time *The Late Late Show* started, he was asleep. The dog too. There was no one to talk to except the talk show host. Nothing to look forward to except a prize, perhaps. A week in New York. A Five Star Hotel. Ten thousand dollars to spend. She punched the answer onto her Nokia mobile, immobile phone, and waited. Who will you bring? The talk show host might ask. My husband, she'll tell him. My partner.

She was used to the long absences; the empty house; the week broken up by book club meetings. She envied the other women, husbands at home, children tucked into bed. They needed a break they said, some 'me time'. Maeve had all the time in the world. One of the advantages of being married to a man who travelled long distance for a living.

"The best of both worlds," Ev would say, her blueberry blue eyes conjuring up more positions than the Kama Sutra.

"Weekends must be so exciting. Like falling in love all over again. Are the chandeliers still intact?"

Maeve didn't remind her friend that they had ceiling spotlights; couldn't tell her she was more alone when he was there.

Saturday was for chores, 'we' time for Jack and Maeve. A trip to Woodies, coffee in The Happy Pear, a stint in the driving range, even though she didn't play golf. There was no underage soccer practice for them, no forests of dirty knees and hockey sticks piled into the car, no teenage girls banging doors, no birthday parties with castles bouncing in the back garden.

The tests had been torturous and didn't reveal anything, except disappointment. Jack had refused. "No one's gonna mess with my tadpoles," he'd said, his voice low, resolute. "Unless I say so."

Sunday she got him ready for the week ahead again. She emptied his suitcase and was throwing his smalls into the laundry basket when it hit her. She'd organize a foursome. Arrange to meet Ev and her husband for drinks in Mrs. Robinson's some Saturday. Sit at a table together, chatting, elbows touching. Like a real couple. Like partners.

She decided to weed out his wash bag. It would be blue mould by now from tops off the toothpaste, spilt after-shave and soap cracking with age. Something was stuck in the corner, shrivelled-up and gooey, sticky to touch. She tweezed out a condom with two perfectly shaped red nails. She'd never seen one before.

Used.

Woman's Way February 2014

You Could've Been
Someone

"Jesus!" Dan gazed out the aeroplane window at a Wedgewood blue sky. "So this is what Ireland would look like without the clouds?"

"Do ya think I'll get in?" was all Rob could say.

"Of course ya will." Dan pressed the button for the Air Hostess and ordered two bottles of Harp. "Might as well start as we mean to go on."

"What if I'm turned back?"

"You won't be," said Dan, but he wasn't so sure. He'd applied for a J1 at the last minute. His Uncle Martin said they'd been clamping down big time since 9/11, taking fingerprints and photographs of your eyeballs. They could take all they wanted, Dan was taking no chances.

"I have to get a job," said Rob.

"How come every other moron in Ireland is making money," said Dan. "But your old man is losing it?"

Five hours later, he was grabbing the gear bags off the carousel along with a hurley stick belonging to Rob. He'd never played the game, but Martin had said it was a sure ticket into New York. Dan had an internship and his magic boxers in his bag, they were all the tickets he needed.

"Have a nice day." Rob slapped him on the back.

"Ya got through?" When Dan saw his friend, he was sorry then he'd spent the extra few bob on the Visa.

On the Airtrain, the hurley hopped off the sliding doors, the Perspex windows, the passengers perched in their seats, the airline personnel slick in their uniforms. On the subway, it nearly got them killed every time it poked some dude in the peanuts. The carriage was hot and rattling, reeking of cologne and mouthwash, heaving with body fat and hip-hop. When they stepped out into oven that was Brooklyn, they fucked the hurley into the nearest dustbin.

"Let's find Flanagan's," Dan said, sprinting across the street, following Martin's directions. The barman had two cold bottles of Becks propped up in front of them before they'd even dropped their bags. There were many more varieties of American beer, they discovered, as well as shots of Sex on the Beach and Slippery Nipples.

"I think I'm dying," Dan looked up from the toilet bowl where Martin found him on his way home from work. "I'm vomiting blood."

"That's the grenadine, ya gobshite."

They cashed in more itinerant cheques, as Rob was calling them and started on the Fuzzy Navels after that. "Here's to itchy bellybuttons," Rob said and Dan nearly died laughing.

Martin and his mates kept playing *Fairy Tale of New York* on the jukebox and it only fucking June, roaring along with the Pogues, still in their work clothes and dusty boots. Every now and then, they jumped off their stools, leapt into the air shouting out the words, arms outstretched every time, punching the air with their fists, every voice in Flanagan's joining in.

They think it's about them. Dan stood there, gaping.

"Pathetic," Rob kept saying, his face streaming sweat. "Mammy must've forgotten to send them the fare home."

But, Dan could remember Martin playing football with him before he went away; queuing with him for hours to see *ET*; taking him to the pantomime at Christmas; buying him his Star War and GI Joe figures when he come over first; bequeathing him his old Dandy and Beano Annuals. Dan still had a picture of the two of them beside his bed.

"Meet me outside in a few," Tommy the barman whispered, tilting his head towards the door. Tommy Clean they'd been calling him because he never stopped wiping the counter. Once outside, he produced white powder rolled up in dollar bills. Dan couldn't be got off the dance floor after that. He was surrounded by a circle of American girls smiling like mad to get at him.

Next morning, he woke up beside this one.

"I'm Missy," she said, as soon as she opened her eyes. "Nice meetin' ya." She rolled off the couch onto the floor. "See ya around," was all she shouted from the door.

"God Bless America," said Martin on his way into the living-room. "Now get into that shower and be ready in twenty minutes."

"Why, do I smell that bad?" Dan rubbed the sleep from his eyes.

"Because you're going to work, dick head. What d'ya think you're here for?"

"Well, I thought I'd have a holiday first?"

"Not a chance," said Martin. "The boss is expecting you at nine."

"What's for breakfast?"

"A can of Coors, if you're lucky."

"How about Rob?"

"He'd better start looking." Martin sounded different than he remembered. There was an edge to his voice. Still in construction after ten years might do that to a man, still renting an apartment. "A day without work is a day without a dollar," Martin said.

Dan stepped out onto the sidewalk a couple of hours later and had to crane his neck to see the sky. This is more like it. The sea of yellow cabs, the whirr of bicycles, the pedestrians pressing towards him on Wall Street, this is it. He bought a paper cup of coffee from a lad in a caravan and strode towards the AIG building.

"Welcome to Corporate America," said his superior on the sixty-fifth floor, gripping his hand. "My name is Chuck and I don't give a fuck."

Rob got a job as a bar-back in Flanagan's and was making as much as Dan after tax and social security was stopped. He had a rake of women lined up every night when Dan strolled in from work. And the *craic*, there was loads of it, crack cocaine too, his new lady love. Dan thought he was king of the world, Superman and GI Joe rolled into one; he thought he'd won the lotto; that every day was his birthday; that he'd died and gone to Heaven.

"And I'm never going back,' he'd roar over the crowd every night in Flanagan's, Rob responding with a thumbs-up.

Chuck said he was hot shit, pushed him all the way towards a bonus, kept telling him he was a valuable asset to the team. Dan started thinking of a year out from College in Dublin, stepping onto the real bandwagon that was Wall Street, maybe even get Chuck to finance him to finish his Degree at NYU.

"We wanna get back to the eighties," Chuck would tell the team, "back to when we were lighting our cigarettes with dollar bills."

Jesus. Dan would nearly start smoking, just to try that one.

Rob took up with a girl they called Piano Legs, because, that's right, you got it, and she introduced Dan to more than just her girlfriends. There was Ketamime, Qualudes, MDMA and Molly, much nicer names altogether.

Then, Rob's mother rang at five o'clock one morning, just as Dan was starting to think about getting up and he only in bed a couple of hours and this one beside him and his head throbbing, and his gut about to heave onto the floorboards. "What time is it over there?" he asked her.

"Nearly midnight," she said. "Can I speak to Rob?"

Dan rolled off the couch, staggered down the hall to the cupboard Martin called a spare room and saw the empty bed. "He's not here," he said into the phone. "Try Flan's."

"I did," said the mother. "He didn't turn up tonight."

"Wha'?" Dan couldn't get his head around that one, couldn't get around much these days. He was in trouble all the time with Chuck don't give a fuck, and with Martin who had dollar signs for eyelashes. Couldn't make it into work some days, couldn't rid his brain of the fuzz. There's no 'I' in team, Chuck was suddenly fond of saying, looking at him funny.

"He hasn't turned up this three nights," she said. "Haven't you seen him?"

And it dawned on Dan that he hadn't. That hadn't happened the whole ten years they'd known one another.

"Tell him to give me a ring." The mother sighed. "His Dad's not well . . ."

"I will."

"Who was that?" said Melissa, or Lori or Cookie, or whatever the fuck her name was. Imagine calling someone biscuit?

"Nobody." He gathered up her clothes from the floor. "Time to go home."

He called Flanagan's and Tommy Clean told him Rob was fired. He called Martin on the job and he told him they were both out on their ears. He called Piano Legs who rang around the hospitals and found Rob in a Jewish Medical Centre of all places. Well, they had a guy fitting Rob's description unconscious from an overdose, she said, and Dan should get over there straight away.

After making a stop for coffee and a packet of paracetamol, Dan strode into the hospital in flip-flops, a muscle shirt and shorts. A nurse gave him scrubs and showed him to Rob's room. When he heard the blip-blip of the screen and saw the tubes dangling from his friend's nose, his mouth, affixed to his arm, Dan cried himself into convulsions.

He spent the next twenty hours listening to the slow rhythm of Rob's breathing and remembering the day they became friends in Tiny Tots Montessori. Rob's eyes as round as saucers when he saw Dan's GI Joe collection, when he heard Dan had an uncle in Brooklyn. 'Swap ya for a Spiderman,' Rob had said and they'd been swapping ever since. 'You and me will go to America someday,' the little blond boy would repeat over and over during their games and with the help of GI Joe, they'd dream themselves already there. 'We'll live in a skyscraper.' Rob's imagination grew with the years. 'And we'll make millions of dollars and drive around in a big Rolls Royce.'

"God Bless America," Rob said when he woke up the next day and Dan could've kissed him.

When Rob was discharged, Piano Legs took him to Martin's to pick up his bag, his passport and the few dollars he'd managed to save.

"I have to go home," he said to Dan. "My Dad is after dying."

"Jesus," was all Dan could say.

"Yeah," said Rob. "He did it to himself, it seems."

"Don't they all?" Martin shook his head.

The words whirled around in Dan's head and he couldn't speak. *He did it to himself?* His insides were in a knot, as he watched Rob slouch down the steps of the apartment building and disappear into an awaiting cab. He hadn't the heart to ask him for the rent.

"It's your own fault," Martin said when he threw him out. "I don't mind the drink, but those drugs are a different thing altogether."

"Fuck off," was all Chuck said when he fired him.

Dan stepped into Rob's shoes as bar-back then; slept in the store room above Flan's most nights and with Piano Legs when she was in the humour. He snorted a fair share of the tips up his nose and still managed to leave the overdue rent for Martin, Rob's share too.

He fastens his seatbelt and looks out onto Manhattan, a necklace of shiny jewels. He's sorry in a way he hadn't made more of the summer, made his mark on the city, seen some sights, said goodbye to Martin and got a reference from Chuck the Fuck.

God Bless America. He snaps shut the window. He won't be back any time soon. It's 2008 after all. There's plenty of work in Ireland now for young bucks like him, the Banks throwing money at them, no need to immigrate anymore. Fuck that. He presses the button for the Air Hostess. May as well start as he means to go on.

He looks at a card on the table in front of him. *You are someone* it says on the front, *to me* on the inside. He hadn't been able to decide who to send it to, so he kept it for himself, in the end.

June 2013

Just Memories

WHAT'S IN A NAME?

My name is Frances. Growing up, I didn't like my name, until I heard its history. On a beach in Kilkee, my grandaunt Nan told me that my grandmother was also Frances. I knew that. Her mother was Frances too. I may have known that. What I didn't know was that her mother, my great great-grandmother, was Frances Knapp, a young Welsh woman who married Paddy Bourke, a merchant seaman from Limerick. She died giving birth to her only surviving child, on January 12th, 1867, in Cardiff. This little Frances was taken back to Ireland by her father when she was four years old. All of a sudden, I like my name, and now, I'm interested.

I picture her in a velvet dress, lace collar, red wavy hair, fearful but determined on a voyage across the Irish sea and then a train journey perhaps all the way down to Limerick. Her Aunt Kate, more like an older sister, teaching her how to sew and sing. After Kate's marriage, Frances moving in with her Uncle John at 38, Athlunkard Street, where she stayed until her death eighty-two years later. John Bourke, an itinerant gardener, travelling the countryside, his niece in tow, tending the big houses. They spent nine months in Kilrush once, the housekeeper teaching her how to mend frayed carpeting, paving the way for a job later in Cannock's on William Street.

I see it as a lonely life, the slip of a girl and the red-bearded man, no one but strangers for company. And home teeming with people. The street filled with a host of uncles, aunts and cousins, real and honorary. Girls skipping rope on the pavement, the boys kicking a rag ball around the road, sing-songs at Broderick's corner.

Frances Bourke was twenty-two when she married Paddy Lynch, a baker by trade, keen fisherman and rower, one of the co-founders and the first captain of Shannon Rugby Club. They had nine children, six of whom survived, and when he died in 1915, "we had nothing," Nan said.

His widow opened a huckster shop in the front room. Sat on the stairs of a summer's evening with her pals, Madges Turner and Quinlivan, watching people walk out to Corbally or take the Charabanc to Plassy. Over then to Murnane's in the morning with the cracked jugs, back after dinner to collect them, warm with milk. Into Jim Packet's after Mass for the tripe and trotters, home then to feed the family, one of whom had been christened Frances.

"Your grandmother was the most like our father," Nan continued. "She played the violin just like him and she'd his lovely thick hair and she'd the features and all of him and his smile; his quiet and gentle nature. She was a great dressmaker too and that's what she worked at after she left school."

In 1922, she married Con Browner, wearing a tan costume with a chain belt, and a cream kind of a pale yellow blouse, crepe de chine. The reception was held upstairs in Thirty-eight, the two Madges providing the breakfast, wedding cake and all. The Best Man, Dinny Lanigan serenading them with *Mother Mo Chroi*, but never getting further than *There's a spot*. Someone shouting, "Where's the spot, Dinny?" Their honeymoon interrupted by Civil War bullets, as they lay on the floor of a Dublin tram.

The newlyweds settled in Thomondgate, hiding a man on the run from the Tans in their attic, Con reporting on GAA and politics for the Limerick Leader. Frances returning home to Athlunkard Street every day with one or other of her seven children. My father Connie eventually deciding to stay altogether, such was the pull of the Parish.

In later years, it was into the Savoy, mother and daughter, to see the latest film and to hear Connie sing at the interval. If the picture was good, they'd stay for the second show. To heck with their tea those nights. Granny Lynch in a long black coat, her Baby Power and ball of snuff hidden deep in its pockets, always a sixpence for a visiting grandchild, waiting at the door for letters from America, from children she never saw again.

My grandmother, Frances Browner, died in 1951, aged fifty-six. Her mother, Frances Lynch, ordered laurel leaves for her grave because laurels, she said, were for champions. My father bestowed the same bouquet on her coffin in 1956. Granny Lynch's namesakes in the family today are Frances Lynch-Gravelle, Arizona; Frances Spalding, Edinburgh; and me.

Ireland's Own January 2015

HAPPY BIRTHDAY BLOOMSDAY

All of the planets were in disarray the day I was born. Only that one of my houses rested firmly in Cancer, I might have flown into orbit altogether, the fortune teller said. At some stage during my mother's twelve-hour labour in Cork City, however, an event occurred in Dublin that would place the date forever in literary history. Five men met in Sandycove, where the book begins, to retrace Leopold Bloom's footsteps through Ulysses. John Ryan, Flann O'Brien, Patrick Kavanagh, Anthony Cronin and Tom Joyce gathered at the Martello Tower where they engaged a horse-drawn cab and set off across the seafront.

On the 16th of June, 1954, Bloomsday and I were born.

Three months later, my parents embarked on their own odyssey to Donegal, Sligo and Offaly before finally settling in Dublin in 1962, the year the Tower was renamed the Joyce Museum. Growing up in Glenageary, we were a stone's throw from Sandycove where Buck Mulligan held his shaving bowl aloft and within walking distance of Dalkey, the setting for the schoolroom scene in Nestor's Episode.

Yet, I didn't encounter Joyce until Inter Cert English. The young boy in Araby, infatuated with a girl on his inner-city street, stirred the Romantic in me; his eyes burning 'with anguish and anger' when he failed to find a trinket for her in the local bazaar. Sister Raymond had me read the story aloud to the class because I put so much feeling into it, she said. I devoured the rest of *Dubliners* after that and when Gabriel watched his wife grieve for a deceased former lover in The Dead, I was filled with an awful foreboding that all is not fair in love. In UCD, I read *A Portrait of the Artist as a Young Man* and was introduced to Stephen's stream of consciousness and Joyce's epiphanies and the writer's desire to 'forge in the smithy of my soul the uncreated conscience of my race'.

After graduation, I worked in the Allied Irish Banks, in Aer Lingus and as an au pair in Paris, before heading to New York for a summer and staying twenty years. A poster of Joyce's Dublin brightened up my bare Bronx wall. 'FROM SWERVE OF SHORE TO BEND OF BAY' the words blazed above pictures of my homeland; sapphire blue waters and sunny place names and the author's assurance that if Dublin was ever destroyed, it could be rebuilt from the pages of *Ulysses*. It was in New York that my love affair with my birthday began. I heard Fionnula Flanagan recite Molly Bloom's soliloquy on Broadway and was transported home by her Dublin accent. In 2004, I returned for *Bloomsday 100*, donned a lace vintage dress and a string of pearls and tipped it down the road to Sandycove. Sipping coffee outside Caviston's, I heard a man in a straw hat remark, 'it's the only country in the world where a date in literature is celebrated.'

And it's my birthday, I whispered.

During my stay, I attended lectures in the National University of Ireland on Colonial Joyce; Transcultural Joyce and even Excremental Joyce, but it was the Dublin outside the College door that captured my imagination. The pseudo-cobbled streets of the IFSC were buzzing with prosperity, teeming with young people who looked confident, content even, in a way that had been out of ken for their predecessors.

It was time to come home, for good.

In a one-minute video of the original Bloomsday, the sun is shining, as an artist, author, two poets and a dentist jostle into the cab at Sandycove. Ma would have been in the Erinville Maternity Home delivering her first child and Da popping into a telephone kiosk on Patrick Street to hear 'it's a girl!' The men in the movie are in a merry mood, singing and smiling, relieving themselves on Sandymount strand and stumbling outside the Bailey, where they abandoned the pilgrimage, it seems, for more drink.

"It was the happiest day of my life," Ma told me before she died.

I live in Greystones now but it is to Sandycove I will return on the 16th of June, in my vintage lace and pearls. I will stand on the low granite wall at the Forty-Foot where Da used to swim every single morning of his life there and I will look across at Howth Head and say 'yes' to my Universe. 'Yes I said yes I will Yes.'

Happy birthday Bloomsday.

And happy birthday to me.

Sunday Miscellany June 15, 2014

A Kings' Town Again

My mother used to tell us that she always stood on deck until Dun Laoghaire was a dot in the distance. A small bus would have rattled out of the Midlands earlier that day, her suitcase tied with twine to its roof. The train took her from Dublin city to this south county port and once disembarked, she followed the crowd, she said. Everyone back then was bound for the boat to England.

A row of Georgian houses flanked the seafront; Killiney Hill hovered in the background; Dalkey Island lay resplendent to the left. There were no cranes or modern marinas, no glassy apartment blocks. The two Church spires would have been visible and the Royal Marine Hotel, but not the shopping-centre sandwiched in between. Ma's last glimpse of her homeland was an unknown terrain, as unfamiliar as the country that beckoned.

On a holiday home, however, she met a handsome Limerick man at Shannonbridge Carnival and never went back. After seven years of marriage and several stints around the country with the ESB, my father found work in Forestry and put down roots in Dun Laoghaire. Ma's view from the kitchen sink then was the two piers embracing the harbour, the mail boat gliding across Dublin Bay and Howth Head seeming so close, we thought we could touch it with our fingertips.

The Dun Laoghaire of my childhood was a bustling town. Bandstands throbbing with music, the Baths heaving with swimmers, staggering lines clamouring for a cone outside Teddy's. I went to the pictures for the first time in the Pavilion to see *Pollyanna* and mitched from school once to watch *Gone with the Wind* in the Adelphi.

As a pupil at St. Joseph's on Tivoli Road, I marched down Patrick Street for the Friday sodality; for my First Confession and First Holy Communion and for my Confirmation in a pink suit. A year later, 1965, I watched in horror from Killiney Hill, as St. Michael's became engulfed in flames.

The town was thronged with English tourists that time. Women in flowery dresses and beehive hairdos and men who talked like the *Two Ronnies*. My brothers and I bested each other counting colourful Ford Consuls, Austin Martins and Morris Minors, their Jaguars zooming up and down Marine Road.

Alas, the Seventies saw the end of these exotic visitors, as the Troubles in the North escalated. Towards the end of that decade, though, the shopping-centre was opened and Dun Laoghaire thrived again. You couldn't walk a few feet of a Saturday without bumping into someone you knew and a quick run into town often turned into a social marathon.

By then I was clerical officer, permanent and pensionable, with Dun Laoghaire VEC and spending all of my wages in Norah Barnacles and the Elphin, Smith's on Cumberland Street and the Lesley Inn. Wednesday night was Peekers for ninety-nine pence beers and seagull stew; being able to smoke in comfort and not having to worry about the drive home. Sure, we could always walk or hitch a lift anyhow.

One day, I hopped on a 747 instead of the 7A and for the next twenty years viewed the town through the lens of the returned immigrant. Home on holidays, my first ports of call were always a trip to the shopping-centre, a walk on the pier and a photograph on the blue bench at its farthest tip. I would sit at our kitchen counter, drinking tea with Ma and looking out over the Bay, imprinting the scene on my memory to take back to noisy New York streets and sprawling suburbs.

Now home for good, my soul aches when I see shop fronts boarded-up, businesses closing down and the shopping-centre a shell. The heart has been torn out of the town. But, I have hope that Dun Laoghaire will rise again. Look at the sparkling seafront, now a hub of artistic activity with the Theatre, Town Hall and People's Park all celebrating Arts and Letters. Let us welcome the new library to our skyline, to Ma's long ago last glimpse of home. Let us believe that Dun Laoghaire can be a Kings' town again.

Wheeling Dad around Dalkey recently, I asked him what had brought them here over fifty years ago and for the life of him, he couldn't remember. Possibly its proximity to Wicklow, we decided, and his work in the lush forests there.

"Whatever the reason," I told him, "you picked a beautiful part of the world for us to grow up in."

"Did I?" He looked at me, his eyes glazed with wonder.

Yes, Da, you did.

Ireland's Own February 2015

THE AMERICAN PARCELS

We always knew when an American parcel had arrived. We could tell the minute we walked in the back door from school. The kitchen would be in disarray with papers, coloured strings and packages scattered across the floor. Exotic aromas of vanilla and musk mingled with Ma's soap powder and baked bread. Her reddish-brown curls flopped onto her forehead, a smile beamed from her lips and she chatted nonstop in an octave higher than we were used to.

My heart would skip at the sight of the two tiers of cardboard standing three feet high in the middle of the room. There would be clothes spilling out of boxes, draped across chairs, flung on the floor. And there was always matching outfits for me and my two sisters.

Green velvet pinafores with pearl buttons and collars of cream lace. Red corduroy ones too with white blouses underneath, which we wore in the family snapshot at Christmas. Daffodil cotton dresses and straw hats with yellow ribbons announced the arrival of springtime. We wore them to mass on Easter Sunday, clutching American prayer books in our podgy fists, as if we were marching down Fifth Avenue in the Easter Parade. Floral anoraks brightened up summer showers and duffel coats carried us through tough Irish winters. Once, I got a pink watch with a pink strap, which I showed off when raising my hand in Mrs. Griffin's fourth class.

Pandora would have been envious of such treasure – rows of chewing gum falling onto our laps like an open accordion; gooey sweets and candies sticking to our teeth with delirium. Betty Crocker cake mixes in mysterious hues of blue and green, far more preferable than Ma's homemade scones and tarts.

Best of all were the sugared ice cream cones, but alas no ice cream, much to my brother, Gerry's, chagrin. The flavours suggested on the cartons, however, made us yearn to fly off to that golden land, which offered such delights.

Auntie Nan had immigrated to America in the forties, even though she already had a job in her native Limerick. Her sister, my grandmother, encouraged her to go, hoping she'd meet new people and get away from minding the growing number of nieces and nephews. I would love to have met my Granny, after whom I'm named and of whom I have heard so much. She must have been so kind to give this advice to Nan, whose help she was in need of. Was she hoping she'd find romance too?

Reality was a factory assembly line and sharing a one-bedroom apartment in Sunnyside, with her younger sister, Maureen, who was married with two children. "Mau was the pretty one," Nan used to say. "Your grandmother was the singer. And I was the plain Jane," she would sigh.

How she must have missed the block of terraced houses on Athlunkard Street and the bells of St. Mary's Church across the street, which pealed through the slumber twice a day and brought the inhabitants to their knees for the Angelus. What would she have given to pop in next door to Cissy and Brigid for a cup of tea, or have Nellie Bourke stop by, or Rosie Gleeson and did she promise a million times that if she could only be transported back for one day, she would never again scold Jack, or correct Fanny's kids when they ran around the house, or used the wrong basin for the dishes, or made a mess at the table when they were eating?

The little street would be packed on a Sunday morning with Mass goers, and again on a Saturday night for confessions, and on a Friday evening too for the Sodality. And her door was always open and she could have a chat and admire a new coat or hat, or remark on the fact that they had the same one now for a long time!

Eventually, Nan headed West for California and landed in Hollywood, where she became housekeeper for Father Lawlor. He provided her with a studio apartment, a salary and a trip home every two years on the Holland-America line, which took six days to cross the Atlantic Ocean before it docked in Cork. Because Nan refused to fly.

She'd arrive with a doll in a box, a red coat, my first pair of Levi's and a pink and white polka dot dress, which I wore to my first real dance. There were pictures of tanned American cousins with blond hair and braces and the sun was always shining. Newspaper cuttings pronouncing graduations, proms and weddings were stored in a wooden box beside Granddad's bed. I couldn't wait to get there.

Meanwhile, Nan would interrupt our television programmes to point out some celebrity she had shown into Father Lawlor's office. She was on first name terms with Bing Crosby and his family; had met Gene Kelly and even stood in line behind Mae West at the supermarket. Before we knew it, she'd be gone and we'd have to wait for the next letter, the next bunch of photographs and better still, the parcels.

When she was sixty-five, Nan retired and returned to Limerick. The homestead on Athlunkard Street had been demolished and she was given a house by the Corporation. She thanked God every month for the Social Security cheque, most of which was spent on sending parcels back to the American cousins.

To celebrate her 90th birthday, we threw her a surprise party in Shannon Rugby Club. "I'm going to have a heart attack," she cried when she saw the crowd. At last, all of her nieces and nephews and their children and grandchildren, from both sides of the Atlantic, were united in her honour. She received greetings from President Clinton via her grandniece, Carol, whom he had appointed head of the Environmental Protection Agency. Nan, in turn, sent a Waterford glass paperweight to Al Gore, whom she had met in Shannon Airport when he was en route to Russia. 'How's Zachary?' she asked after Carol's son, showing no interest in the Vice-President's speech about problems with the ozone layer.

"I'm going to get a phone," she announced during the week-long festivities. "So that I can ring ye all when ye go back!" She'd been reluctant to do so up to then, in case anyone called when she was out.

I once asked her why she spent so much of her money on us over the years. She told me that when all of her brothers and sisters got married, neither she nor her mother could afford to give them a wedding present and she had never got the chance before they all died. Instead, she is parcelling it out to their families while she's still alive.

And alive she is and kicking. "This old body might have let me down," she'll tell you. "But my mind is as clear as an eighteen year old!"

East Hampton Star 1996

Nan died in 2002 at the age of ninety-seven. Fifteen years earlier, I had followed in her exiled footsteps. Long Island boulevards, no more than Hollywood hills, were not caked in gold and it was only then that I realized the sacrifice it took to pack those long ago parcels. Rummaging around department stores like Ohrbach's and Sear's, dispensing of hard-earned dollars, Auntie Nan realized her American dream by bestowing bliss on faraway Irish children. At what cost to personal fulfilment?

& Ireland's Own 2013

THE CARNIVAL GIRLS

I went to my first dance in Cloghan Carnival. The Friday night céilí it was and I all of fourteen years, in a purple empire-line my mother had made me. We set off up Castle Street, my cousin Alice and I, turned right at the square, which is now a roundabout, where we fell in with a few girls from the Hill Road. Another two or three we picked up on Banagher Street and by the time we reached the fork in the road for Birr, we were a giddy group. The chat was all about which lad they had their eye on for the evening, and whether they'd 'go' with one of them later that night or not. Looking back, that was the best part. The camaraderie and casual friendships that weave the fabric of a small country town were denied to me in Dublin.

Heading for the Sports Field, we could hear the tinny strains of fiddle strings, a tin whistle and piano accordion. We could smell the turf smoke, even though it was July; crunch the grass under our cube heel shoes; see the Marquee soar majestic towards a royal blue sky.

I had never been 'asked up to dance' before. What would I do?

I lined up along one wall with the women, that's what I did, and ran away every time a surge of men made for us. For, men they were, aged sixteen to sixty and all agog. I took solace several times in the ladies' loo, sitting despondent on a bale of hay, while a frenzy of females jostled in front of a postage-stamp mirror. Their sweet perfume mingled with toilet odours and the smell of sawdust.

"Why didn't ya bring yer knittin'?" one lad had the nerve to shout in at me.

Alice was having the time of it, twirling around the floor for the two-step; quick step; slow waltz and the jive. In and out and in and out and in and out for the Siege of Ennis. Her younger sister, Marie, popped her head in, along with the three children she was babysitting. You'd find all sorts at a ceili. Catching my forlorn face in the corner, she gasped. "Did ya not get a dance yet?"

I was beside meself.

Finally, I sought refuge in the cloakroom, where the attendant promised to mind me. An elderly woman, I thought, and dependable. Thanks be to the Lord God. I was about to relax, tapping my patent toes to Brendan Shine's *Bridges of Paris* when a burly farmer approached, red faced and freckled, a tweed cap clutched in the huge hand he proffered.

"Will ya dance?"

I nudged my cloakroom companion.

"Say no," she whispered and I obeyed, filled with guilt for letting him down, worried that he might feel rejected. But, no sooner had the word fallen from my lips than he'd whisked HER out on to the floor, whirling HER away from me. Never saw a sign of them since.

Next thing, a nice-looking lad appeared, his face shiny and hopeful, his hand clammy when he took mine. We were getting along fine until the end of the set and I didn't know how to take my leave of him. I had forgotten to ask Alice, you see. What was I to do? He tilted his head towards the floor and we danced again. And again and again. Panic started to set in. Couples were meeting and parting all around us and after seven sets, I felt faint. What would he make of me? The Girl from Dublin. A Hot Bit of Stuff. The only heat I was feeling was around the Peter Pan collar of Ma's homemade dress. Eventually, Alice ended up beside us, turned to her partner all smiles and said, 'thank you.'

Thank you?

As easy as that?

"Thanks a million," I said to my lad, who looked like he'd been hit with a hurley.

I couldn't be stopped after that. Tripping across the floorboards. Sweat steaming. Faces and lights rotating. My heart lifting with the music, falling for the National Anthem. Alice and I running all the way home laughing, the start of many such nights, the tea and currant cake left out by Auntie

Peg. The two of us, then three of us, four of us, five, according as her sisters started out, sitting in front of a dying fire, reliving dance after dance after dance.

During the day, we practiced our steps around the kitchen. I would carry a portable record-player down on the bus all the way from *Bus Áras* and we'd jive to The Tremeloes' *Suddenly You Love Me*, waltz to Larry Cunningham's *Don't let me cross over* and for the two-step it was *Shoe the Donkey*.

The season started in June with Ferbane; July was Cloghan; August we had Birr Vintage Week and Ballycumber; September all roads led to Banagher. The tent pitched beside the Shannon, waves rustling, the moon shimmering above the bridge. If you got off with a Banagher boy you were made up. With their leather jackets, long hair and revving motorbikes, they were the fine things. And, with a bit of luck, you might wangle a date for the Donkey Derby.

In the winter, we had to make do with the dancehalls. Standing on the square, thumbs out for Birr, Ballinasloe, Athlone or Tullamore. All of Ireland's main arteries flowed through Cloghan, you see. Or, we could pile into the Bennetts' Ford Consul for the price of two shillings. Packed in with another nine or ten maybe. Sardines would have been sorry for us. More sins were surely committed on that journey and we couldn't do a thing about it, Father. Alice had to sit on the radiator in the Central Ballroom once, to steam the creases out of her black bell-bottoms.

The only place open on Christmas night was Quigley's Hall in Banagher. How I'd envy Alice and Marie and I home alone in my bedroom, dancing every step in my head. Next day, I'd be on the train to Clara, in time for the County Arms on Stephen's night. One year, there was no bus to Cloghan. "Do you know anyone around these parts?" The stationmaster scratched his head, not knowing what to do with me. My mother's cousin, Rita, and her husband Jimmy Keenaghan? His eyes lit up. He took me to their house straight away and Jimmy later drove me all the way to Birr for the dance.

In the seventies, the carnivals stopped. The discos came along and the hotel nightclubs, but we still had the cool showbands like Derek Dean & the Freshmen; Rob Strong & the Plattermen; The Conquerors and The Memories. Ah! The memories. It was at the *céilí* it all began; that first Friday night in Cloghan. And after turning up the hem of my new empire-line for the following Friday, I never looked back.

"Life in the Midlands long ago was mundane," Marie recalled recently. "The carnival with the lights and the music and the people coming in from everywhere was a huge thrill."

I know Marie, I know. Wasn't it the same for me? Didn't I cross the country for it? Trek eighty-two miles on a train and a bus and even hitch lifts from auld lads to get there?

Banagher Review 2014 & Sunday Miscellany June 2015

CHEEK TO CHEEK

"A rugby pal of mine, Young Munsters' coach Mickey Cross, always impressed on us to tackle cheek to cheek. It was the safest way, he said, to topple an opponent, safer than a head-on collision. I learnt this to my dismay when playing with Birr RFC back in 1953."

My father arrived in Ferbane in November '51 to survey sites for the proposed new Power Station. It was a pleasant enough evening, with shards of autumnal sun still evident, when he disembarked the bus on the Belmont Road. His instructions were to pick up equipment at the local Garda station. A handsome young man of twenty-five, with a shock of black shiny hair, he cut a dash, as he swaggered through the sleepy town. On rounding Hiney's corner, chance stepped forward in the form of Jimmy Madden. Within an hour, he had not only located his kit, but had found digs above Chapman's sweet shop and an assistant.

A city boy, he knew little about the country; but as a Munster man, he knew all about rugby. Eventually, the two would wed. "In a country place like that, the club finds you," he told me. Destiny despatched fellow Limerick native, Des O'Brien, to fetch him. A teacher at Birr Vocational school and a player with the RFC, Des succeeded in signing on the new recruit. Dad togged out the following Sunday and playing rugby for Birr was one of the highlights of his term in the midlands.

"A car would collect me every week and take me to Birr, or whatever town we were playing that day. We togged out in Egan's Hotel there on Main Street and played in a pitch behind the Esso station. After the match, we would return to the hotel for a wash and the lads would drink a few pints while I tried to start a singsong. That night, the club fed me hillocks of homemade brown bread, cold roast beef and tea I could trot upon, before driving me back to Ferbane. There was no training, as far as I know, I never had to train anyhow. Maybe they considered me something of a star because of my history with Shannon and Garryowen!

We had some great games and to top it all, I met a girl called Sadie Bell and we became engaged three months later. Things could not have been better. An incident occurred then that could have caused me to give up rugby altogether, or take to the drink. Thank God, I did neither.

It was a crisp, March afternoon when Birr were advancing towards the 1953 Provincial Towns Cup and we were playing against North Kildare. About ten minutes before the end of the first half, one of our forwards caught the ball at the end of a lineout, broke away and ran diagonally across the field. He eliminated the scrum half and I spotted an opening.

Calling for the ball, I took the pass, straightened up and sprinted as hard as I could towards the try line. I was the out-half, the last man on the line, and it was the first time that day I had a chance of scoring so I was making the best of it.

Suddenly the gap closed and this lad came in to seal it off. He lunged forward, about knee high and challenged me head on. It wasn't cheek to cheek you see and I caught him with my knee on the forehead. I was travelling at a terrific speed and soared out over him, tumbling for about five or six yards, before hitting the ground with force. By the time I stood up and returned to check on him, I knew he was hurt. He was snoring, eyes closed, and although there wasn't a mark on him, he seemed stunned. When he bared his teeth, we saw droplets of blood and took him to a nearby cottage hospital. Forty minutes later, he died.

We went back in a daze to Egan's. They wanted me to have a brandy, but I didn't. I had a cigarette instead even though I had given up smoking for Lent. The Guards took me to the station for a statement, a desperate ordeal altogether, and the North Kildare lads agreed it was an accident. Our team attended the removal and funeral in Summerhill, which was very sad. The deceased's girlfriend had been at the match and his brother was playing. A nice farming family they were, losing a son like that must have been heart-breaking.

Birr withdrew from the cup, but North Kildare organized a replay six weeks later and insisted that I line out, arguing that if I didn't, I would never play again. So I did, even though my heart wasn't in it. They beat us and went on to win the Cup. The ESB transferred me to Cork at the start of the summer and after that to Donegal. I was gone for four years before returning to survey a site for the Bord na Móna plant at Derrinlough and went straight back to Birr RFC. Two Harrington brothers had joined up, and Fitzer, a local lad who was mad keen. Every evening after work, the four of us would meet to practice the 'scissors move.'

Harrington would pass me the ball from the left and I would run across the field. Fitzer advanced from the right, cut back and I would turn and switch the ball inside to him. He would cross behind me and head for the try line, as I ran forward. We were travelling in opposite directions like the two tangs of a scissors. The idea was that by the time the opposition realized I didn't have the ball, Fitzer would have scored! After drawing with them twice, we beat Navan with that move. Years later, I met a man from the Board of Works. He was on the Navan side that day and cursed our 'move.' He said he saw what we were doing, but couldn't do a thing to stop us!

I was back in Birr one time at the wedding of Sadie's niece, Yvonne Dolan, to Seamus O'Brien of Kinnitty. In Dooly's Hotel the next morning, I spotted a fellow who looked familiar. By any chance, I asked the waitress, is that Fitzer. I don't know, she shrugged, his name is Gerry Fitzpatrick. Did he ever play rugby I inquired? I couldn't tell you, she smiled, but he talks about nothing else. Sure enough, it was my old friend, Fitzer, and we spent the morning reminiscing about rugby. We could have spent the whole day, he was that keen, and remembered every kick of the ball. He had even taught our 'move' in later coaching sessions, he said, assuring his young squad that it always worked for us!

When Birr broke up, I was moving to Dublin and in my thirties so it was time to pack it in. And I had six children, three of them prospective young players. In fact, two of my sons, John and Gerry, played with the Birr President's XV team at their

Centenary Fixture in 1987. It was an honour for them to be playing for their father's old club and in their mother's county.

Birr RFC was the last club I played with and, as a result, I look back on my time there with fondness. Great camaraderie, great rugby, great friends. It always brings to mind Mickey Cross's coaching call – always tackle cheek to cheek. I learnt the hard way that he was right."

Every November, for the past fifty-seven years, Brendan Coleman's name appears on Da's List for the Dead. This story is one we grew up with and as children our favourite part was 'cheek-to-cheek'. As an adult, I realize now how harrowing the accident must have been for him, for his team and for his club. I can see them huddled in O'Brien's bedroom that night, young men in their teens and twenties, heads down, shoulders hunched, gazing into a smoky haze, bewildered by Fate's first cruel blow. Their concern for a friend impossible to articulate. Their grief at a player's passing too profound to express. Their love for rugby forever marred by this memory.

"There was no cleaner player than Connie Browner," a team mate told me, "a gentleman to his fingertips. After the collision, Connie dropped the ball and ran to Coleman's aid. He didn't even dream of scoring."

In a letter to his father, dated 12/3/1953, Da wrote: *The Birr lads could not have done more for me, staying with me all evening and Des O'Brien even made me stay with him for the night. His landlady, Mrs. Hackett, was very kind, giving me something to make me sleep. The Birr Club had a Mass said for the deceased in my name the next morning and the whole team attended. I had to appear at the inquest after that and I went to pieces again. These last few days have been terrible, but please don't worry about me. Prayer is the only thing now. Brendan Coleman was at Confession on Saturday and received Holy Communion on Sunday. It is consoling to know that God took him in a State of Grace."*

Birr Review 2010

The End, Or Is It The Beginning?

" Where is it?" I asked my sister when she called me in the Bronx in the summer of '87.

"I dunno." Anne was vague. "Just take the train from Penn Station all the way to the last stop."

The LIRR was freezing for a June morning. I curled up on the black plastic seat and fell asleep under a towel, as strip mall USA flashed by the window. Three hours later, the train suddenly stopped in what looked like the middle of nowhere.

Were there lobster pots bobbing among the waves that morning? Bathers on the stony beach on Navy Road? Was there anyone fishing on the jetty that caresses the Bay the way the piers do in Dun Laoghaire? Did an osprey soar in the direction of the Montauket? Did I notice a low flat-roofed house on the corner, beside where the tracks intersect the road? That was to become Mick and Kev's place and a great pit stop on the way up from the beach.

You'd always be sure of a drink of water or a cup of tea or, better still, a beer and sometimes you could end up staying the night, or even a day or two, if the craic was good and there was room on the floor. "Cirrhosis by the sea," George christened it and Bernard declared it the end of an era when the lads left the house last year to go off travelling. We were left wondering where the next halfway house was going to be and most of us thought it would be Tommy's place because he always had the best parties up in Jefferson.

"Don't bother inviting anyone," he'd assure Christine. "They'll all just show up." And, sure enough, we did.

Now, Christine maintains that nobody visits them since they moved up to South Forrest. Have another party lads.

I peered out the window that morning and saw Anne in the distance, standing among the gravel. There was no proper platform; no apparent station-house; no visible ticket office; no sign; nothing. There was nothing to announce the fact that I had arrived in Montauk, the end of the line.

"There's no taxis." Anne greeted me. "We'll have to walk into town."

"That's OK," I said, breathing in the fresh sea air. "Is it far?"

"Nah, we'll be there in no time," she promised.

Today, there would be anything up to eleven cars from two or three taxi companies awaiting our arrival and competing for our business.

'Are all the drivers Irish?' Someone asked me recently. 'Ah! No. We have two Americans,' I said. 'Bonnie and George. We call them our tokens,' I told them. 'Oh,' they laughed. 'We were just kidding!'

Well, it's no joke. Not only are the drivers nearly all Irish and the majority from Dublin, but Montauk boasts seven Irish female drivers among their taxi force. Well done girls!

By the time Anne and I had reached the gazebo on the green, I had fallen in love. Thus began a love affair that has endured nine years, fourteen jobs, a couple of heartaches, a host of wonderful friendships, countless goodbyes and endless laughter. A love affair with a place such as I had never experienced before.

We passed the Manor magnificent on the left and to our right were the waters of Fort Pond glistening like diamonds in the midday sun. I was to see those waters turn emerald, sapphire, an icy steel grey and black. I would see them frozen over in winter and bathing in orange at dawn and sometimes in the summer, on the way home from breakfast in Salivars, I would see Fort Pond turn pink and purple and even bright red too.

We passed a white boarded building jutting out into the Pond, its shutters flapping in the breeze. We would come to know it as the Lakeside, the Place and finally the Auld Shebeen. In the summer, you'll often catch Dave hauling crates of empty beer bottles out onto the deck; the windows and doors wide open to let out the fumes of stale cigarette smoke and beer dregs. If he sees you – beware! He'll surely slag you about what you got up to the night before when the place was rocking to the sounds of DJ John. If you had to leave your car behind, the whole town will know it, and it will be a cause of speculation as to why you couldn't drive home or where you spent the night.

Half the time, it was probably Dave's fault, as he'll insist on a shot or two and he loves to top up your drink when your back is turned. Although, as Bonnie says, 'Did he tie your hands behind your back and force it down your neck?' No, but he would if he could.

Anne and I stopped for breakfast in the Seabreeze. "The waitress is Irish," I whispered.

"I know, they all are," she informed me.

"But, how do they get here? How do they know about it? I was flabbergasted.

Well, they hear about it in the Universities and Colleges at home. In the student union offices and in USIT in New York. They hear about it from friends who've been here before and from brothers and sisters. They stumble on it from East Hampton and Amagansett. Some of them stay on the train and never get off. They arrive in droves, white-faced and tired, laden down with backpacks and full of expectation.

'D'ya think we'll get a job?' they ask hopefully. 'D'ya know of any accommodation?' They're polite and they're friendly, ready for work and wide-eyed with innocence. They're full of gratitude and everything is "brilliant!" They're away from home, sometimes for the first time, making money and free to do whatever they want.

"The night life is excellent," one of them told me. "One hundred percent better than Cape Cod last year."

The first crop of Irish strolled into town around 1981/82. Some of them didn't bother leaving after the summer ended. They lived in a group of houses down by the Sands Hotel, which they called Glenroe. Tommy came out for the weekend to get away from his aunt in Valley Stream, found a job landscaping and stayed. Hilary was visiting Tommy, met Paul and within a week had decided to marry him. 'I'd rather take a slow boat to China,' Paul is reported to have replied.

Bernard reckons there were about eleven or twelve of them around the bar in Surfside in the winter of '87. Maria thinks that's the year she and Annemarie came too. They lived upstairs, cleaned the rooms, bussed tables, mixed salads, served breakfast, lunch and dinner, washed dishes, helped prep in the kitchen and fought over their only pair of leggings when getting dressed to go down to the bar every night. There, they drank California sunrises, played pool and snogged someone beside the fire before crawling back up to bed again for a few hours' sleep until the breakfast shift began.

If we were to congregate together today, we reckon there would be about fifty of us. There must've been that many at Kelly's christening last year and at Janette and Gene's engagement. And easily that amount at Maria's surprise 30th birthday party when Mick maintains we got a better crowd than Black 47.

And why do we stay?

Well, we stay for the work and the money and because the people are nice. We stay for the long, hot summers and the walks around Fort Pond. We stay for sunrise in the Montauket and the crazy nights in Shagwong. We stay because we have businesses here and have started families. We stay because we don't know where else to go. We stay because we love it and because there is nowhere we'd rather be right now.

We stay until the landscape is an artist's canvass, splattered with yellow and gold, green and rust. We stay until the leaves fall off the trees. We stay for Jimmy's dinner at Thanksgiving and Tommy's birthday in December. We stay until the Christmas lights go up in the gazebo and Santa comes to White's. We stay until the snow falls in January and before we know it, it's Paddy's Day again and we're talking about summer again, and without realizing it, we've become year-rounders. 'The sand gets in your shoes,' according to Nancy. 'And you just can't shake it out.'

Anne and I wandered down to the beach after breakfast. "I wonder what it would be like to live here," I said.

"I dunno." She was already setting her towel down on the sand. "Probably be boring."

"Yeah, you're right." I lathered on the baby oil. "Grand for a holiday," I said. "But, that's it."

"That's it," she said.

Montauk, the end. Or is it the beginning?

Montauk Pioneer, July 1996

A Long Walk For Love

We were swerving all over the Saw Mill River Parkway, ninety-four year old Joe hugging the steering wheel; his wife Rose in the back seat; me beside him holding on to my hat, if I had a hat, as we careened off Exit 19 for Irvington.

"We'll have a look at the Famine Memorial first," Joe declared, pulling into the VE Macy Park, a swath of green and lake water.

Rose and I clawed our way out of the maroon Mercury Cougar. "How are you now?" she whispered, a cheeky grin curling the corners of her mouth.

"Fine," I said, trying to steady myself, my feet glad to be touching solid ground again.

On a warm May evening, full of sunshine and birdsong, we picked our way through the park to the sculpture at its Western end. Five figures cast in bronze are leaving the ruins of a cottage. Four of them look forward, while one emaciated face glances back at opposing gable-end walls; all that is left of his home. A fallen wicker basket, or creel, is full of potatoes that turn into human skulls, as they tumble to the ground.

"We'll be having our own Memorial," Rose eventually broke the eerie silence, "if we don't eat something soon."

Joe drove slower this time towards Molly Maguire's – his favourite Irish restaurant. "Because it reminds me of home," said the man who hadn't lived there in nearly eighty years.

I had been interviewing him all week about his coming to America when he was seventeen and how he couldn't figure out the amount of milk on the boat and not a cow in sight. The first day I called to his house on the Bronx River Road, we spent seven hours recording his memories. About how he was born the day the Titanic sank; about the two-room school he had attended in County Clare where they had to bring a sod of turf every day for the fire. About the time the Master tried to send one of his classmates home for misbehaving and the young lad was adamant: 'I'll not go 'til me turf is burnt.' How a passing cyclist had roared into the yard at them, "Michael Collins was shot."

How the boat had docked at Pier 59 in Manhattan and as soon as he was settled in the grocery business, Joe took accordion lessons for a dollar an hour and spent the next sixty years in *ceili* bands playing for the Irish all over New York State. How he had met Rose at one of these dances in the Carmelite Hall on 55th Street, when she marched up to the stage and demanded *the Stack of Barley*; how he knew after three dates that he wanted her to be the mother of his children.

That day in her home, she would offer me tea; I would decline. She'd put on the kettle anyhow and minutes later I would have to turn it off. Our recording is interspersed with the whistling kettle and rattling of china, yet I managed to consume fifteen cups of tea in the course of my stay. Joe had explained to me that his wife wouldn't be able to take part in our discussion, how her memory was long gone.

I was preparing to leave when she grabbed my arm and said, "I came over in 1932, the year of the Eucharistic Congress, with a cousin who'd been home on holiday."

I grappled in my bag for my digital voice editor, pen, notebook and glasses, as she proceeded to recount her days as a waitress in a downtown restaurant, her life as a young wife and mother of five children whose husband was away a lot, how she knew that Joe was solid from the word go. She described her homesickness for family and her trips back to Leitrim to see them. "I'd have been a spoilt cat if I'd complained," she finished, and then returned to the living-room, leaving me in the hallway, spellbound.

'Don't ever switch off your recorder,' I advised my Oral History seminar at NYU's Glucksman House.

After that, she spoke sporadically, but was unable to verify facts or enlarge on particular aspects of her life, if questioned. Nevertheless, I included Rose's story in *While Mem'ry Brings us Back Again*, a collection of immigrant memoirs I compiled for the Aisling Irish Community Center in Yonkers. Her children were amazed, not having heard some of these reminiscences.

"My mother was from Mohill," she suddenly announced after our roast beef dinner that evening in Irvington. I quickly smoothed out a paper napkin and had my pen at the ready. "And my father from outside Drumshambo," she continued. "He used to walk the twelve miles there and back every day to see her." Rose's blue eyes sparkled remembering. "Wasn't that a long walk for love?"

Sunday Miscellany May 2015

UNDER CLERY'S CLOCK

Home on a holiday from New York ten years ago, I took two Greek Americans on a tour of Dublin. This was their first visit to my native city and I was eager to impress. Starting at Heuston station, we ambled along the lovely Liffey banks from where historical monuments were viewed with a murmur of admiration. Christ Church Cathedral rose from the heart of medieval Dublin towards a baby blue sky; the dome of the Four Courts surveyed the now booming city from its granite throne; Viking ghosts tramped Wood Quay on that sluggish summer afternoon. My guests were unmoved.

Crossing the river at Grattan Bridge, we burst onto the kaleidoscope that was Capel Street, amid a musical explosion of Caribbean calypso and Nigerian juju. One Kodak moment was missed when a lofty, dark man wrapped in brocade, approached my friend, Kyprios, for directions. Another was neglected on Moore Street, where its famous fruit and vegetable market resembled an oriental bazaar, offering exotic spices and wriggly eels alongside the 'apples and oranges' of my childhood.

After strolling onto Daniel O'Connell's wide thoroughfare, I ushered my party into the GPO to see the bronze statue of Cuchulainn. This effigy of a mythical Irish hero, after whom our Golf Society in the Bronx was named, failed to pique much interest. Exasperated, I swept my arm across O'Connell Street in the direction of an elegant grey-stoned edifice. "There's Clery's," I said, "under whose clock Irish couples have been making dates for over a hundred years. In fact," I added for embellishment, "it is the setting for maybe a million love stories."

"Really?" Elena, the other half of my entourage, perked up. "Let's go see."

She spun around and strode across the street, stomping past the sophisticated Spire – our 'stiletto in the ghetto' - turned on her own spiked heel at the top of Talbot Street and marched towards Dublin's most distinguished department store, just as its two-faced familiar square clock struck eight.

"Look! Somebody's waiting." She pointed at a solitary female slumped against the broad shop window, her eyes darting to and fro in hopeful expectation. Seconds later, a gangly youth ran forward and gathered her into his arms. My chic New Yorker squealed with delight. Whisking out a disposable camera, she snapped the unwitting couple, thrilled to have finally found a landmark worth recording.

"Did you ever have a date here?" She arched a pencilled brow at me.

"Why, yes, I did." I recalled a rugged, red-haired Donegal man, whom I met at the Ace of Clubs dancehall in the early seventies. Our appointments were always UCC, where he would present me with a bar of chocolate and insist on paying my bus fare, even though I had a weekly commuter ticket and could travel for free. There was a brawny Offaly man, whom I met every Monday night UCC throughout the summer of '82. We had no contact the other six days, but once a week, without fail, I would wander up from the 7A bus stop on Burgh Quay to find him under the clock awaiting my arrival. When he decided to give up on city life and return to the Midlands, I missed our balmy Monday night trysts.

The Greeks were charmed with my memories and despite more sightseeing stops at Trinity College, the statue of Molly Malone's 'tart with the cart' and a pint in Davy Byrnes, the highlight of their trip turned out to be 'the date'. It was a wonder to them in this high-tech age of text messaging, email, and cellular telephone, that trendy young Dubliners were still using an old-fashioned arrangement for getting together.

In 2006, I came back for good, and it took me a full two years to feel part of the landscape again. Since then romance has bloomed, once more with an out-of-towner. Our courtship is conducted long distance, and entails many hours driving up and down the N4 and M50 motorways. To curtail travel time, we sometimes use public transport and socialize in the city centre.

"I'll meet you under Clery's clock," my newfound friend suggested the first time we considered this option.

And I was home.

Clery's Valentine Prize & Ireland's Own September 2012

Remember Me To Inquiring Friends

My grandfather kept a wooden box beside his bed. For me it was a treasure trove of pictures, newspapers cuttings and letters from my English and American aunts and uncles, cousins and second cousins. When I eventually met these exotic creatures, it was as if I had known them all my life, for, of course, I had. On visits home, some of them would take mementoes from the box, to keep as souvenirs. In 2011, my father and his six siblings met for their final reunion. Auntie Betty from California brought back letters she had previously confiscated from the box. They were from a Kate O'Gorman in Philadelphia to her mother in Limerick. In one of them, dated February 8th 1878, Kate wistfully declares, "Mama dearest, if only I could write, the stories I could tell.'

While compiling a history of the Browner/Lynch family, my father's cousin, Con Cowhey, came to my aid. He had in his possession a bundle of letters from a Conductor Cornelius O'Gorman of the Army Commissariat Department of East India, to his mother in Limerick. He has to be Kate's brother, I decided. The earliest is dated December 1849 from Warley Barracks in Essex and the next was written in 1860 from Delhi where he was a Warrant Officer on a salary of £120 a year. Up to 1885, Cornelius remits regular dispatches and always encloses a money order in the amount of five or ten shillings. He inquires after a list of aunts, uncles and cousins by name and is concerned for his sisters, Honora and Margaret, and their children. Remember me to inquiring friends he signs off some of these epistles, promising to visit within a year or two.

The letters present us with a first-hand account of history. Cornelius refers to a 'failure of the potato crop again' in Ireland; the Phoenix Park murders that leave 'a black stain on the country and its people' and a famine and fever in India, which took the life of his first wife and an eleven-year-old daughter.

In 1860, he warns younger brother, Patrick, that 'without education he is nothing more than a slave.' In 1872, he hopes and trusts that 'poor Patrick will succeed & prosper in America' and in 1874, he reports that his brother 'is seriously thinking of coming to India, as trade isn't good in Philadelphia where he is now.' But in 1877, Cornelius writes, 'I am sorry to learn that you have no account of Patrick.' In 1880, 'I cannot understand how it is that Patrick does not write' and later that year: 'I am of the belief that if he is alive, something or other prevents him from writing.'

In one of Kate's letters, she states: 'I have not heard from Patrick in over a year, he was in California then.' She later determines never to marry as her sisters 'had such poor luck' with it. One of them, Honora, was widowed young and had a daughter, Lizzie Kelly. Kate also signs off: 'best respects to all inquiring friends' and promises to return home 'if God spares my death another year or so.'

Correspondence from both of them ends abruptly in 1884 and a memory card announcing the death of Margaret O'Gorman in 1885 indicates that she is their mother. As I already knew that Lizzie Kelly was my great-grandmother, I realized that Cornelius was my great-great-granduncle and Kate my great-great-grandaunt. Margaret then was my great-great-great-grandmother. And despite her children's promises, she never saw them again.

A crumpled sheet of paper in Granddad's box reveals an obituary that appeared in the Limerick Chronicle, February 1902:

'The Pioneer of India says – Major O'Gorman passed away on Christmas morning (his 70th birthday) at his residence, Gormanston, in Dehra Dun, his cheery presence as familiar as the trees and the villas of the stations in which he served. Imbued with a deep love of his native Ireland, his heart diffuses some of her sunshine around others and many a quaint story is told of him.

He entered the Hon'ble East India Company's Forces in 1849, joined the 2nd European Bengal Fusiliers and served throughout the first Burmese War. In 1857, he entered the Commissariat Department and was present at the storming and capture of Delhi, where he had his shirt 'literally riddled with bullets.' He served in the Bhutan Campaign and throughout the Afghan War and retired in 1884, 'after topping the head of his department, and completing 35 years of service, all in India.'

And I see a man looking at his mother's likeness in which he 'tried to recognize even a single feature but could not.' Hear his grief for a poor sister who was obliged to go into the workhouse and a brother who disappeared. Have him take 'a look at the Taj Mahal' while acknowledging the Agnes Dei and sewing needles she sent him from a small city in Ireland.

'What a pity India is so far away,' Cornelius writes, 'so as we could all live together and be happy as we might wish to be.'

I see a woman tearing open the flimsy envelope, pulling out the order for the dirty shillings, as they were known. Hear him promise 'never to forget me parents.' Have her shed a tear. Want to whisper in her ear that he 'thought so lightly of his heroic acts that he never received the Victoria Cross to which he was clearly entitled.'

So, it was with immense interest that I read Ferdinand Mount's article: *Aunt Ursie's ripping yarns of the Raj* in the Sunday Times, March 1st 2015.

In it he describes the lives of British ex-pats in India and wonders how they endured the long separations. Not only from their homeland, but also from offspring whom they packed off to boarding school at an early age. My Uncle Cornelius had two wives who bore him six children, all of whom were sent away before they were eight years old. Mount refers to the 1857 Mutiny of India, where terrible atrocities were committed by the British Army to suppress the natives.

A quick glance through his letters reveals that in 1862 our ancestor refers to an 'Indian Medal & Clasp for Delhi, earned five years ago.' The dates do indeed concur. The earlier image of his bullet riddled shirt occurred at 'the Subzi-Mundi, a strong masonry village held in force by the mutineers.' Is it possible that great-great-grand Uncle Cornelius, after whom my father, grandfather, brother, cousin and nephew are named, was not so great after all? Could a loving, dutiful Irish son have been merciless in his dealing with others? Then again, slaughter and mass hangings and murder would've been carried out by both sides in a War. But, Uncle Cornelius?

My grandfather, Cornelius Browner, had made his own inquiries. A letter to him from Independent Newspapers, Fleet Street, July 1939, encloses an address for a Col. P.W. O'Gorman in Middlesex, who would have been Patrick, Cornelius's eldest son. A letter to Granddad from that address states, 'it is now one hundred years since the late Major Cornelius O'Gorman left Ireland and further interest for us has long ceased.'

When I first read this, I thought the reluctance was because of snobbery on their part, or the desire of Cornelius's family to distance themselves from Irish ancestry. Now, I wonder if it's something else altogether. Did the O'Gormans want to detach altogether from their association with India's Raj? The era that left a lasting stain on Britain's history, according to Ferdinand Mount. A subject that former generations hardly ever mentioned; one that they preferred to skip altogether, he believes.

And I think of the brother and sister so far from home, missing their mother, always mindful of siblings and relations. Who knows what Cornelius had to do to provide for them?

Kate O'Gorman's unwritten stories or her brother's ripping yarns? To think of all that we have missed.

March 2015

WE WENT TO A GARDEN PARTY

The highlight of last year was Uncle Paddy's 90th birthday party. Things started to roll in February when Kieran Ted posted the invitation on Facebook and Auntie Phil from Philadelphia replied: I'll be there. Cousin Ann from Connecticut came a close second. By March 1st, I had my flight booked.

On the last week in June, all roads led to Nuneaton. We were flying in from Dublin, Denver, Shannon, Boston, Philadelphia and Toronto and Paddy's son, Brendan, his five children, wife Sally-Anne & mother-in-law, Avril, were en route from Sydney via Dubai. We were driving down from Inverness, Edinburgh, Liverpool and London and travelling by train from some of those places too. We converged at The Chase Hotel, Higham Lane, on June 28th, for a memorable family weekend.

Patrick Joseph, the first of seven, was born July 8th 1923 in Limerick City, to Frances and Con Browner. The four boys were educated by the Christian Brothers on Sexton Street and at the age of fourteen, Paddy joined the Order as a Novitiate. Wanting to participate in the foreign missions, he headed for St. Joseph's College in Ledsham, across the Mersey from Liverpool and was to spend the following eighteen years as a Brother. "I suppose England is foreign," his brother Eamonn remarked.

`After graduating from UCD with a Degree in English, Latin & History in 1944, Paddy was allowed his first visit home to Limerick. The second was when his mother died in 1951 and for Paddy, going home was never the same again. He left the Order in 1955 and met Mary Donaghy whom he married the following year. They have five children: Sean, Brendan, Brigid, Siobhan and Kieran. When Paddy retired, he was Headmaster of St. Thomas More RC Comprehensive School in Nuneaton.

As his sister, Maura, was born after he left, the first time the siblings came together was in 1944. The next time all seven united was in 1992 for his daughter, Brigid's, wedding. Since then, there have been four more reunions, the last one was in Limerick in September 2011. Sadly, his brother, Michael, died in Miami in December 2012, so there will be no more meetings of this 'magnificent seven'. However, it is heartening to know that their children, grandchildren and great-grandchildren will continue the tradition, as was obvious in June when first and second cousins from all over the world mingled, as if they had known one another all of their lives.

The first glitch in proceedings was a Facebook announcement from Randy Robinson on Wednesday night that Auntie Phil's flight had been cancelled because of weather and she would be arriving in London instead of Birmingham. By the time I logged in the following morning, Joe Galloway was already on his way to Heathrow. *How marvellous,* I wrote, *what you've managed to arrange through Facebook in a few hours?* Joe messaged me that Facebook had not done a damn thing; it was he who had saved the day, with an identikit photo and a large sign shouting PHIL.

The next SOS was from Brendan looking for Ann Murray Robinson's mobile number. He was at Birmingham Airport, but could not find her and had made several overhead pages. He asked us to text or email her that he was standing outside the Spa market.

'Let the fun begin,' Michelle Cross comments and Lisa Jackson-Heaney safely at home in California, remarks: 'oh gosh, the adventure of it all!'

We were relieved to see Kieran's post Thursday night: *All the wrinklies are accounted for and sitting in Mum and Dad's. Everyone is talking and nobody listening. Dad asleep.*

Friday night, we gathered at Brigid and Alan's for food, wine, a wee dram of Drambuie and the requisite sing-song. Saturday was Sports Day on Ennerdale Crescent, with fierce competition for trophies and shouts of 'middle, middle middle' during the three-legged race; followed by fish 'n chips in the back garden and an ice-cream from Mr. Whippi. Then, it was back to The Chase for night-caps.

The grand event took place on Sunday at The Chestnuts Club on Old Hinkley Road when the sun shone all day for our Garden Party. The finale was a pub quiz, which exposed the Browner cheating gene, and an all-hours game of charades.

The best part was bumping into Browners everywhere: shopping on Bridge and Bond Streets, watching the Lions beat Australia in The Chase and wandering along Higham Lane. Brendan wrote on Facebook that he was pleased to see the family trait of never saying a nice word to a relative if you can think of two unpleasant ones is alive and that the volume each individual could create, even 'the quiet ones' like Barbara, is still louder than a 747.

In this era of Nintendo DS, X-Factor, the X-Box and I-Phone, ten-year old Paul Gavin from Limerick regarded the trip to Nuneaton as 'ex-cellent'. Paddy, who still calls Ireland home, is an ardent supporter of Limerick hurling and Munster Rugby - *There is an Isle, a bonny isle.*

Ireland's Own June 2014

POLLYANNA

My sister, Barbara, came home from Philadelphia with the idea. She'd been there for the summer of seventy-nine, staying with Auntie Phil and Uncle Pat Murray on Sansom Street. On the third of July, a neighbour's grandson, who had six hundred pounds of dynamite in his basement for fireworks, lit a cigarette and blew three houses on the block to bits. Speeding away in an ambulance, Phil saw her house cave in; the curtains flapping through a window, and remembered her charm bracelet left behind.

Barbara, meanwhile, was busy in Smokey Joe's, working as a waitress. On her way home on the trolleybus, she heard the sirens; saw the emergency services; noticed the crowd thickening as they approached her stop. "I live here, I live here," she cried, trying to break through the strip of yellow tape that cordoned off Walnut Street. Finally, a friendly police officer came to her aid and brought her to the station where she found Phil in her bare feet, covered in dust. Their daughter, Ann, was undergoing eye surgery, and Pat organizing a place to live.

They spent the first night in a Salvation Army Hostel, the second in a Holiday Inn, moved in with friends for a while and eventually settled in a studio apartment on nearby Walnut Street where the family would live for the next year. By the time the neighbours were buried a couple of days after the explosion, my uncle's hair had turned white; they had lost everything.

Barbara was without her passport, clothes and jewellery, and whatever money she had squirrelled away over the summer. She continued working in Smokey Joe's and took refuge in the home of a colleague.

"How do you manage Christmas?" The girl's mother asked when she heard of her seven siblings.

"We don't," said Barbara.

The woman proceeded to explain the concept of Pollyanna, whereby everyone buys one gift, for a name picked out of a hat, the giver remaining anonymous until the gifts are exchanged.

When Barbara related the idea to the family on her return home, we agreed to give it a go. In the early days, when we all lived at home, Pollyanna took place on Christmas morning in Glenageary. Gradually, as birds fled the nest, we started having it in our respective homes, taking turns each year, the date changing.

Out of twenty years in America, I only missed two Christmases at home, but the name of my Pollyanna was mailed to me, a present dispatched and one received. The only year we skipped was 2009, the year our mother died, because Ma just loved Pollyanna.

I still have the pink and white striped dressing-gown she gave me the year I left and the electric kettle and toaster for my new home when I came back. The Newbridge cutlery from John when I moved to Yonkers and Neil's two paintings of West Cork that have adorned the walls of every home I've had since. The green 'Billy bag' is still a favourite accessory and a leopard print scarf; pearls and a beaded purse. *Brendan Behan's New York* still sits on my bookshelf, but numerous gifts didn't stand the test of time – I recall a white frilly blouse, worn to a thread and gold earrings from Dubai, only one of the pair now intact.

The first gift I received, a vintage Vogue mirror, hangs in my bathroom today, but I doubt that the vinyl Boomtown Rats LP that I bought for my brother, Michael, has survived since 1979. And I know for sure that the Little Red Riding Hood notepaper, purchased for Barbara by baby brother, Paul, in the sweet shop across the road, has been shred long ago.

Our family history can be traced through these gifts and although Kris Kringle and Secret Santa are now popular, for us it will always be Pollyanna. The idea has been adopted by extended strands of the family and even the grandchildren eagerly await the day that only the adults get a gift.

On December 29th this year, I will host the occasion in Greystones, where twenty-three of us will gather to celebrate this Christmas ritual. Surprise guests will include our cousins, Brendan and Sally-Anne Browner, all the ways from Sydney, Australia.

The Murrays eventually moved back onto Sansom Street, to a different house, as the site of their previous one was by then a community garden. They celebrated fifty years of marriage in 2008 with a party in Phil's native Limerick, where their charred passports and scorched wedding pictures were displayed, alongside her new charm bracelet.

They will never forget America's Birthday and we will never forget Pollyanna. Because of an unknown woman in Philadelphia, whose name we don't remember, our favourite family tradition has endured thirty-five years.

December 2014

Mr. Charlotte Bronte

Born in 1816, Charlotte Bronte was destined for the lot of most Victorian women - 'a nightmare of poverty and self-suppression,' she called it. She was the third daughter of Patrick Bronte, an Irish curate, and his Cornish wife, Maria. The family lived in the austere parsonage of Haworth, a steep hill-village with dark, cobbled streets on the edge of the Yorkshire Moors. Within three years, Maria died of cancer and the two eldest daughters of consumption. The remaining siblings became immersed in a fantasy world of their own creation. Charlotte, Emily, Branwell and Anne dreamed up romances and intrigues peopled with rich and powerful characters more vivid than any their restricted world could have encompassed. "We wove a web in childhood," Emily wrote, "a web of sunny air."

This web was torn in 1831 when Charlotte was sent off to Roe Head School, an elegant establishment managed by Miss Margaret Wooller. Her friend, Mary Taylor, records her arrival "in very old-fashioned clothes, looking cold and miserable. Shy and nervous, she spoke with a strong Irish accent." Charlotte's sharp intellect soon took her to the top of the school, where she became assistant teacher. She felt oppressed at Roe Head, however, as she did in subsequent Governess positions, and after a brief sojourn in Belgium, she returned to Haworth, where she recorded in her journal, "I am just going to write because I cannot help it."

Galvanized by Emily's poetry, which "stirred her heart like the sound of a trumpet," Charlotte completed her own collection of poems and four novels - *The Professor, Jane Eyre, Shirley and Villette* and published them under the pseudonym, Currer Bell, his/her sex and identity the subject of speculation in literary England. Thackeray said of *Jane Eyre*, "It is a woman's writing, but whose?" Her assumed surname, however, was taken as a joke from her father's new curate, Arthur Bell Nicholls, who although born in Antrim grew up in Banagher, County Offaly.

And my mother, Sadie Bell, was from Ferbane, less than ten miles away, where her father was a lock keeper on the Grand Canal. She and her siblings could hop on a boat in Glynn that took them to school in nearby Gallen. Their neighbour would hitch a lift on the Guinness barge and partake of a few pints by the time he got to Belmont. I can remember helping Granddad push open the large lock gates and a passing boatman throwing me the odd sixpence; squealing when Dad reversed the car, for fear he'd drive into the Canal; its lapping waters lulling me to sleep at night; a book at my bedside - *Jane Eyre* maybe – for I had grown enamoured of the feisty orphan girl who yearns for 'all of incident, life, fire and feeling.'

The Reverend Bell Nicholls fell in love with her creator. Having received Holy Orders at Trinity, in 1845 he was appointed curate to Patrick Bronte in Haworth. Here, he found a family still bereft from the death of their mother and two older sisters. Branwell caught in a downward spiral of drink and depression, the three girls writing up a frenzy.

It took five years for the tall, bearded Arthur Bell to propose and when Charlotte refused, he pursued her relentlessly until his unbridled passion piqued her interest. After her beloved brother and two sisters died in quick succession and she was left alone with Papa, Charlotte finally consented. On June 29th 1854, they were married.

He took her on honeymoon to Cuba House in Banagher, home of the Royal School where his Uncle Alan was headmaster and where he had boarded since the age of six. "Though remote," Charlotte wrote, "Banagher was by no means dull. Friends drove long distances to visit each other, on outside cars or in phaetons or landaus. Sometimes the young people would start dancing, and Mrs. Bell was often at the piano. There were picnics on the river, everyone had a boat, or could hire or borrow one, and there were concerts. In all amusements, the officers from the barracks in Birr and Banagher joined."

I have strolled those streets, boated on the Shannon there, danced as a young girl in the dancehalls and carnivals; and visited my Aunt on Cuba Avenue. I have Bell relations in Birr, Banagher, Cloghan and Ferbane, but had never considered a connection.

When researching Charlotte's visit to Offaly, I happened on a letter she wrote to her former headmistress, Miss Wooller, the week after her arrival there and one line leapt off the page at me. She and her new husband had been met in Dublin by his brother, Alan, who was Manager of the Grand Canal.

My grandfather, John Bell, was born in lock house #34 at Clonony, King's County, in 1900, where his father John is listed as lockkeeper in the 1901 and 1911 census. When he was sixteen, my grandfather took over lock #32 down the line at Glynn and his brother, Arthur Bell, worked on the tugboats. Their cousin, Peter, who lived in the lock house under the Rialto Bridge in Dublin, traced the family tree back to Balbriggan and had often wondered what had brought his Bells to Offaly.

Could it be?

According to local historian, James Scully, the lock-keeper positions and lock houses on the Grand Canal were always kept within the same families.

"So, are you saying you're related to Charlotte Bronte?" My sister-in-law Gene, was sceptical.

"Maybe by marriage," I told her.

My story is only starting, it seems and is worthy of a sequel.

Charlotte's ended on March 31st 1855, nine months after her marriage. Stricken with chronic morning sickness, she beseeched her husband, "I am not going to die, am I? He will not separate us, we have been so happy."

Six years after the death of his wife and unborn child, Arthur Bell Nicholls returned to Banagher where he lived out his remaining fifty years. He died in 1906 and is buried in the grounds of St. Paul's Church there, a mere four miles from Clonony.

March 2015

BRIGID

Because of the ten-year age gap, my cousin Brigid and I would not have been close growing up. I do recall her visiting Dublin as a teenager and we all thought she was so cool in her dungarees. Then in 1987, she skyped off to Australia and I hurrahed off to America and twenty years later, we both came back. Brigid to her hometown of Nuneaton and me to Greystones in County Wicklow, not too far from Glenageary.

In the summer of 2007, I was working with the Safe Home Programme, recording the memoirs of returned immigrants, and Limerick were flying through the Hurling Championships. On Sunday, August 12th, I had occasion to travel to Birmingham, the same day Limerick were playing Waterford in the All-Ireland Semi-final. Da videoed the match in the afternoon and Brigid and Paddy met me at the airport that evening to pick up the tape. We had coffee, of course, and chatted. I remember being struck by how bright and bubbly my young cousin was, full of smiles and so easy to talk to. I wasn't allowed mention the result of the game, but Da and Paddy would've been on the phone by ten o'clock that night to relive all of Limerick's five goals.

We met again two years later when I was speaking at a book event in the Irish Embassy in London. Paddy, Mary, Brigid and Siobhan attended, and after settling the parents safely back in their hotel, the 'young ones' decided to party. Along with us were more cousins, from my mother's side, who took us on a trail through various vodka bars and nightclubs in Soho. I have a picture of Brigid dancing in one of these clubs with my cousin's son, Shane. The next day, my head like a lump of cement, I rang the Browner girls to see how they were feeling.

"I had imagined us in a Ye Olde English Inn beside a fire," I told Brigid.

"Well, that's what we get for letting a twenty-five year old pick the venue." She laughed. "And what a great time we had," she said. True. It was great fun.

A few weeks later, Brigid took Paddy and Mary to see my mother, who was very ill. I will never forget how kind Brigid was to Ma who had an eye infection at the time, one of the side effects of her chemotherapy. Brigid, switching into nurse mode, helped Ma apply her eye drops and ointments. It was she who advised me to take her to a doctor; that the infection was more severe than it had seemed. And I did. Thank you for that Brigid. And for the lovely letter you wrote to me when she passed away.

In 2012, Kieran and his future in-laws came to Dublin for the Notre Dame-Army/Navy American Football game in the Aviva Stadium and Brigid, Siobhan and Joe came over to join them. We had the usual sing-song in Glenageary the night before the game and that was the first time I heard Brigid's beautiful singing voice.

A colossal spectacle, the event at the Aviva was hailed, but Brigid and I spent the afternoon chatting, hardly glancing in the direction of the football field. It was then that we were christened 'Mary and Sadie' after our mothers who loved to chat too, and drink tea, and sit at warm fires. Their daughters weren't exactly like them, as we liked a drop of the strong stuff in the tea, but we could chat and chat and chat.

The next occasion was Paddy's 90th birthday in July 2013 and what a party that was. What a weekend. What a wonderful family reunion. As Brendan said, we don't meet for years, but when we do, we're mates again. Brigid and I sang a duet on the Friday night, *She Moved through the Fair*, with me providing 'Mary & Sadie' special effects in the background. Brigid moved us with another version of the song on the Sunday.

We were all set for Maura & Tom's Golden Anniversary last June, the same month that we would celebrate significant birthdays. We had even dabbled with the idea of marking the occasion in a spiritual way – Brigid suggested a Retreat, mine was a walk on the Camino perhaps. Unfortunately, she was diagnosed with acute myeloma in March of last year and had to skip the trip to Limerick.

Instead, I went to see her in August and we enjoyed a lovely couple of days, chatting again, shopping in Debenham's and drinking her special brew Italian coffee in her brand new lime green kitchen. We met for the last time in December for Caitlin's 18th and I am so glad now that Brendan whipped us all into going once again to Nuneaton, a place I have come to love very recently.

As well as these wonderful times spent together, many family members also got to know Brigid's quirky personality through Facebook. While many people knock social media, I have found it a great way to stay in touch with family and friends who are far away. And I know Brigid loved it for those reasons too. She enjoyed the banter, the slagging and the craic and was well able for all the wisecracks on the Browner/Lynch page. Her last comment to me was 18th March – *nothing like a lovely reunion.*

Mary and I had coffee in Dobbies Garden Centre on one of those sunny afternoons in Nuneaton last August and we spoke about the special friendship she and my mother had enjoyed. More like sisters than sisters-in-law. "We just didn't have enough time together," Mary said sadly. "Not enough time."

And that's how I feel now about Brigid, we didn't have enough time.

April 2015

POEMS

GREAT STYLE

My mother used to love Lisa Perkins
A boutique on the right,
Right inside the shopping centre;
Monica Peters too, out on the Main Street.
"Wear your style," she'd say to me,
"A woman should always wear her style."

A powder pink top she made me buy
In Blackrock Mall one time,
Egging me back into the shops
Lisa and Monica chortling with delight.
"Treat yourself," she said to me,
"Never be afraid to treat yourself."

The beige cardigan she chose for herself
 With pearl buttons like tears
falling down the front
And the ivory beads lacing her fingers.
"She's so serene," everybody said.
"And always a great one for the style."

STATE OF MIND

Came into work on my day off, she said
The Irish waitress in Clarke's restaurant
Got tired of chewing me nails in the bed
Fretting about bills, how I'll pay the rent
Prefer being here instead of home alone
Serving you steak *sambos* and crispy fries
Nothing to do in this town on me own
Listening to me thoughts, telling their lies
Don't like museums, the movies or shows
Strolling through parks or along Avenues
No love for shopping, in Malls or outdoors
Standing in lines that I used to call queues
I stared wide-eyed at this young girl from Cork
How could she be bored to death in New York?

GRACE'S GARDEN

In a garden in Carrigaline
Trees scrape the sky
Fallen apples cobble the grass
And begonias trellis the patio.
A table and two chairs linger
Beside the silver ribbon of a stream
That ripples the lawn
All the way down to the river.

A crimson red car
Vintage with bulbous spotlights
Lurks under a canvas cover
Its number plate long redundant.
Behind it a bed of snap peas,
Beetroot and garlic bulbs
And a heap of compost heaving
Under the midday sun.

Maisie rushes from the atrium
Curls bobbing about her ears
Jelly legs wobbling
In her Nelly Kelly shoes.
They crush the bruised Bramleys
Lord Lambournes and Pink Ladies
And twirl her around the trees
'til she lands on her bottom, "I dizzy."

I dash to her as I always do
"Let me help you love"
Because I cannot stay away
"I not love," she says, "I Maisie."
Struggling, she stands up
And races towards the river
Behind her breathless in heel-highs
How fast can a woman run?

Past the purple deck chairs
And solitary table
The lattice of begonia and peonies
And sleepy vegetable beds.
Past the shiny red Ford Escort
The air thick with eucalyptus
The car the last of your collection,
The last of you.

On and on she scampers
Alongside the silvery stream
Her little legs hurling her away
"Can't catch me, can't catch *me-ee*!"
My stilettos stab the pea pods
Cloves of garlic and cabbage hearts
My ankles stained beet root
"Come back, come back," I plea.

She stops at the heap of worms
Eggshells and jellied oatmeal,
Soggy tea bags and black banana skins
So carefully composted by you.
"I do a rudie?" she wriggles her nose
And glances sideways at me
Then collapses into peals of laughter
On to the crunchy grass.

"Don't worry, Granny Grace,"
She takes my trembling hand
"I *never* leave you . . .
Don't be 'only . . . I here."
Echoes resound from the patio
"I'll always mind you, Gracie,"
Your hands upon my shoulders
For ever, your eyes said.

The three-year-old girl
And fifty-something woman
Play hide 'n seek and soccer
I spy and Ring a Rosie
Forgotten now the crawling debris
Jam-packed in a pile, festering
Amid the splendour that is
Grace's garden.

Do Chickens Come From Chickens?

Do chickens come from chickens?
Mae eyes the frozen food counter.
I hope so, I say
And a man in Superquinn laughs.

Are my hands really magic?
She claps them as hard as she can.
Of course, I say
As electric light floods my hallway.

Is your Mum really here?
She looks around the graveyard.
That's her, I say
And point out the name Sadie.

And did she used to love me?
Mae scrunches up her nose.
Sure she did, I say.
But, Auntie Frances it's only a stone.

SOMETHING WRONG WITH THIS PICTURE

In Dubai all I saw were eyes
Watching me through almond slits.
Dancing, smiling, blue and brown
I have my eye on you, they said.
Shoes too – tan leather, patent
Sparkly sandals and Jimmy Choo,
Or painted toenails peeping
Under a flowing cotton robe.

The men sat in Malls, their faces free
For all to see, clicking worry beads
Drinking coffee.
They love Russian girls, my sister said,
Who come in busloads to the beach
And sunbathe standing up.

In Birmingham, my cousin collects
His sons from school and women
Avert their eyes, the only part
Of them that he can see.
I have my eye on you, he wants to say
But cannot tell them apart
If in fact he's met them before
If they are the mother of the child
They are claiming.
And then he stops seeing them altogether.

A coachload of schoolgirls explode into the
Food-court where we are sipping coffee.
Teenagers, because of their skittish ways,
Flocking together for a selfie.
An apparition about five foot tall
Or maybe four foot six in high heels
No ethnicity, colour, hairstyle,
Body weight or shape.
Dressed in black, lots of it, forty girls
Disappear in plain sight.

In Florida, everyone drives an SUV
Gigantic tanks of chrome and steel
Advance along the highways
A snake of them coiling around the
Elementary school where children
Wait in line and then disappear
Behind tinted windows.
Eyes can see out, not in.

In Nigeria, one hundred and seventy-five
Million people live on less than a dollar a day
Declares the Irish Times headline
Of Africa's biggest oil producer.
Burnt out bicycles photographed outside
A mosque blasted by suicide bombers.
And that is why Boko Haram will always find
New recruits, the caption continues.
Their faces masked,
Eyes looking out, not in.

MY MOTHER'S HANDS

My mother's hands were healing
Cool against warm foreheads
Steady taking a pulse
Soothing when fevers raged.

My mother's hands were happy
Dipped in flour, kneading bread
Dipped in water, peeling potatoes
Silently joined in prayer.

My mother's hands were cross
Stinging a small girl's legs
That were sore as long as she was
And cured just as quick.

My mother's hands were raw
Red, vessels for rising steam
Bangles of suds at her wrists
Skin crepe paper thin, puckered.

My mother's hands were always
Clad in gloves
Soft leather, fur, sophisticated suede
And rubber.

My mother's hands were white
Lathered in barrier creams
Nulon, Lanolin & Oil of Olay
Her shields.

My mother's hands were freckled
One finger pinched by a thin
gold band. A ring of three diamonds
My father had proposed
On top of a double-decker bus.

My mother's hands never knew
A manicure, until I took her
For a treat. Square clipped nails
Dipped in oil, buffed and varnished
Muscles massaged and kneaded.

My mother's hands couldn't stop
Shaking in the end. I held them tight
Lest the sudden spurts add stress
To a body already wracked in pain.

My mother's hands are still now.

DA

He's fading away in there, they say
Didn't know he was fat until he got
thin
His face pinched up, mouth set in a
line
Is it yourself, he looks at me as if for
the first time

Has to think now before he talks
Like he's trying to remember the
words
Gone the voice always soared in
song
Go jump trenches, scolding us all
the day long

He sits in a chair now, the man
Who swam every day, played
rugby as a boy
Do anything for ya, Marie
said he would
Milk the cows, if ya asked him
if he could

Wanted to dole out his money years ago,
what need had he for it at
eighty-five?
A nursing home I said and was
instantly sorry
Yet his eyes light up now when he
sees me
they say